International Financial Management

S.P. Srinivasan

&

Dr. B Janakiram

Published by:

biztantra

Management for the Flat World!

An Imprint of dreamtech PRESS

19-A, Ansari Road, Darya Ganj, New Delhi - 110 002

Website: www.biztantra.in

Reprint 2008

Printed at: **PolyKam Offset, 257, FIE Patparganj, Delhi-110 092**

Contents

CHAPTER 2

CHAPTER 3

CHAPTER 4

CHAPTER 5

CHAPTER 6

CHAPTER 7

CHAPTER 8

CHAPTER 9

CHAPTER 10

CHAPTER 11

Forward

This book is written in a lucid style, keeping the requirements of students in mind. The chapters have been arranged in a logical manner to facilitate easy comprehension. Student's ability to understand is enhanced by providing illustrations in each chapter and solved model question paper at the end of the book. Case studies have provided necessary practical insight. On the whole this book will serve the felt needs of students, executives and other professionals working in the area of International Finance and will be helpful even to a layman to understand the subject based on self study.

18/5/05

Dr. S. Ramesh

Dean,

Faculty of Commerce and Management Studies
P.G. Centre, Mount Carmel College,
Bangalore-560052

Preface

International Financial Management as a stream has gone through a paradigm shift in the last decade, with Major events like South East Asian crisis and it's contagion effect, LTCM crisis and the role played by OTC derivatives in it, corporate scandals like Enron and Systemic Risk Management devices like Corporate Governance and ALM are the few new issues which figured in the previous decade. The scenario is presently very volatile and many new thoughts are going into it.

This book is an attempt to update the reader with most of the critical issues in International Finance... case studies are given to widen the students' perspective. Illustrations with solutions are given to guide the students. Non mathematical oriented approach and lucidity in explanation is the approach in this book.

If this Book helps a student understand the complexities of International Finance Through self study, the Authors will feel that the purpose of writing the same is fulfilled.

Chapter 1

Introduction to International Finance

1.1 SCOPE OF INTERNATIONAL FINANCIAL MANAGEMENT

After the collapse of the erstwhile Communist Block countries, the world has been dominated by a single super power that is the United Sates of America (USA).This has given rise to what is called as a Unipolar World. Today's world is getting increasingly integrated and the international markets are coming closer to form a Global Village because of the fact that the artificial trade barriers are being dismantled throughout the world.

Today sourcing of capital can be done anywhere in the world and for this Chief Financial Officer (CFO) of an organization should have a good knowledge of International Finance. Apart from the development in information technology facilitated transfer of money at lightning speed throughout the world, emergence of derivative market and big use of the same by speculators has increased transactions throughout the world. Foreign exchange market is a 24-hour market with various centers like Frankfurt, New York, Bahrain, Tokyo, Sydney, London, and Singapore.

India, which had a licensing system for a long period has slowly dismantled the same and customs duties for imports have also been lowered, substantially. Therefore, a firm will have competitors throughout the world in this kind of set-up. Reducing barriers has added significance to International Trade and the study of International Finance is a must for the same.

With huge volumes and expert players, the market has become efficient and because of the change in the attitude towards foreign capital, there is an increasing flow from matured markets to emerging markets. Instruments like American Depository Receipt (ADR), Global Depository Receipt (GDR) facilitate the integration process. The story of derivatives causing extensive damage to International Financial System (as happened in the various cases for example: the case of 200 year old British Barings Bank, which collapsed due to the excessive speculation in Futures by the rogue trader Nick Leeson, LTCM crisis and its subsequent bail out by US Government, huge losses suffered by Procter & Gamble due to derivative trading) heightened the need for increasing awareness about Foreign Exchange Market for properly managing exposure.

1.2 TERMS USED IN INTERNATIONAL FINANCE

There is a Chinese proverb which says that "secret of learning the subject is to understand the terms associated with it" and International Finance is no exception to it. The following table displays various currencies of the world market.

TABLE 1.1 Currencies of various countries.

1.	US	Dollar
2.	UK	Pound Sterling
3.	Australia	Australian Dollar
4.	European Union	Euro
5.	Japan	Yen
6.	South Korea	Won
7.	Indonesia	Rupaiah
8.	Saudi Arabia	Riyal
9.	Russia	Rouble
10.	Sweden	Swedish Kroner
11.	South Africa	Rand

Some of the terms used in the International Financial Management are listed as follows:

1.2.1 Letter of Credit

In International Trade when the buyer and seller do not know each other, the buyer will like to receive the goods and pay for the same while seller would want the payment to be received in advance before he supplies the goods. A bank of repute acts as an intermediary and assures seller that when proper documents as called for in the Letter of Credit are presented then the buyer's bank will make the payment irrespective of the fact whether buyer will reimburse it or not. Letter of Credit (LC) is also called *payment against document* and not payment against goods since the bank's responsibility is to ensure that proper documents as called for in the LC are presented to it and there is no mutual discrepancy among the documents while it is not responsible for the quality or specifications of the goods.

1.2.1.1 Parties to Letter of Credit

The parties which are involved in the Letter of Credit are as follows:

- Buyer,
- opening Bank,
- beneficiary,
- negotiating Bank,
- confirming Bank, and
- advising Bank.*

Buyer

The importer who opens the Letter of Credit, based on the contract he had with exporter, is called as buyer.

Opening Bank

Bank which opens the Letter of Credit based on the request by the buyer

* For the definition of Negotiating Bank, Confirming Bank, and Advising Bank, please refer Glossary

is known as the Opening Bank. Opening Bank will pay the amount irrespective of the fact whether the buyer reimburses it or not. Thus, Opening Bank should be a bank of repute.

Beneficiary

Exporter in whose favour the Letter of Credit is opened is known as the Beneficiary. He can receive payment as soon as he ships the goods based on the documents he draws on the LC.

1.2.1.2 Types of Letters of Credit

The various types of Letters of Credit are as follows:

- Revocable letter of credit
- Irrevocable letter of credit
- Confirmed letter of credit
- Transferable LC
- Back to Back LC
- Red Clause LC
- Green Clause LC
- Sight LC or DP LC
- Usance LC or DA LC

Revocable Letter of Credit

Revocable Letter of Credit can be revoked without the consent of the beneficiary (seller). Because of this, it is not practically very relevant.

Irrevocable Letter of Credit

Irrevocable Letter of Credit cannot be revoked without the consent of beneficiary.

Confirmed Letter of Credit

Sometimes the beneficiary wants the credit of buyer's bank to be confirmed by a bank in his country. This process is called as Confirmation. Confirmation means that the confirming bank undertakes that in the event of proper documents, as called for in the LC being presented, it will make payment irrespective of the fact whether the buyer's bank reimburses the same or not. It charges a commission for doing this.

Transferable Letter of Credit

In Transferable LC, the buyer can transfer a part of the value of LC or the full value of LC in favour of one or more beneficiaries. Transferability should be expressly specified in the Letter of Credit. Since the buyer relies on the integrity of beneficiary, transferability in favour of the unknown person in the Letter of Credit is fraught with risk. Transferable Letters of Credit are taken by middlemen who do not want buyer and seller to know each other and also who want to make a margin without both the parties being aware of the same. Usually transferability in several lots within a single Letter of Credit is permissible but the transferee again transferring the credit is not permissible.

Back to Back Letter of Credit

In Back to Back Letter of Credit beneficiary's banks open several Letters of Credit within the value of mother LC opened by buyer's bank. This is also known as Countervailing Letter of Credit. The terms and conditions of the second Letter of Credit are exactly the same as that of the first Letter of Credit. The second Letter of Credit may be a domestic one. Any change in the second Letter of Credit will be permitted only when the opener agrees for similar change in first Letter of Credit.

Red Clause Letter of Credit

In Red Clause Letter of Credit, advance is provided against the supply of certain documents like drawings and manufacturing schedule as mobilization advance for manufacture of capital goods whose manufacturing cycle time is high. The advance payment is printed in red thereby earning it a name Red Clause Letter of Credit. The bank which provides advance payment has no obligation to ensure that it is used for proper purpose.

Green Clause Letter of Credit

In this type of LC advance is provided against goods, which are manufactured and kept in a warehouse for a buyer against warehouse receipt, before the same is shipped.

Sight LC or DP LC

Sight LC or Document against Payment LC (DPLC) means as soon as the Bill of Exchange of seller is presented to buyer, he should make payment for the same and then only documents will be handed over to him. Thus, no credit is extended to the buyer.

Usance LC or DA LC

Usance LC or Document against Acceptance LC (DA LC) means payment can be made after a particular period from presentation of Bill of Exchange of seller and the buyer can accept the Bill of Exchange presented to him. By DA or Usance LC credit is given to the buyer.

1.2.2 Open Credit

Open credit involves credit offered without any back-up like LC.

1.2.3 Advising

Many a times, LC received from buyer may be a forged one. If the same is routed through a bank, it performs the function of advising whether the LC is genuine or not. For doing this, the bank charges a commission.

1.2.4 Negotiating

Since the buyer's bank opens the LC, payment will be made to the seller only when the buyer's bank receives proper documents as per the LC. This will involve delay like the transit time involved in transferring the necessary documents by the seller to buyer's bank and transfer of money by buyer's bank to the seller's. Negotiating bank is a bank which is in seller's country and negotiates the document presented by the seller against LC. In the event of documents being proper, the negotiating bank credits the proceeds to seller's account immediately, thereby avoiding the delay. For doing this the negotiating bank charges a commission known as *negotiation commission*.

1.2.5 UCPDC

Uniform Customs and Procedure for Documentary Credit or UCPDC is prepared by International Chamber of Commerce, defining the responsibility of buyer's bank, Negotiating bank, Confirming bank, Advising bank and all international LCs bear an endorsement that they are subject to UCPDC 500.

1.2.6 Correspondent Bank

While a bank has to deal in many centers around the world, it cannot afford to have branches in all these centers. It enters into Correspondent agreement with a bank operating in the centre detailing with the scope of responsibilities as well as sharing of the commission. Those banks with which such correspondent agreements are entered into are called correspondent banks.

1.2.7 Nostro Account

The account of a local bank maintained with foreign branch or correspondent is called as Nostro Account.

1.2.8 Vostro Account

The account of a foreign bank maintained with local bank or branch is called as Vostro Account.

1.2.9 Bill of Lading

Bill of lading is a document of Title and is an acknowledgement by the shipper that the goods have been taken by him on board the vessel. A clean Bill of lading states that the package has been received in apparently good condition while *claused* Bill of lading bears notations like package received in torn condition to protect the carrier against claim. Usually, clean Bill of lading is insisted in LCs. Bill of lading can be an *onboard Bill of lading* or received for *shipment Bill of lading*.

An onboard bill of lading indicates that the goods are loaded on to the vessel, while received for shipment bill of lading does not provide any such guarantee. LCs insist on onboard bill of lading. Transhipments clause in Bill of lading generally known as *through Bill of lading* is not generally acceptable to banker. A straight Bill of lading is directly given in the name of consignee. This type of Bill of lading is generally used for shipment to branches or to parties who have effected advanced remittance. The consignor loses control over goods in this type of Bill of lading. In order, Bill of lading is prepared to the order of the banker and unless he endorses the same Title will not pass. This type of Bill of lading is prepared to enable the banker to get the payment first or acceptance of bill first before he endorses and transfers the bill of lading. A *stale Bill of lading* is a Bill of lading, which evidences the shipment much after the contract or LC's specified date.

Charter Parties are closely related to the Bill of lading. A charter party is an agreement entered for chartering a ship. It may be for a voyage for a particular time period.

1.2.10 AWB

Air Way Bill (AWB) is the acknowledgement by the carrier that the goods have been taken on board the aircraft. *House Airway Bill* is issued by air consolidation agent regarding receipt of goods for consolidation, while *Master Airway Bill* is issued by the carrier regarding receipt of goods on board the aircraft. Air Way Bill is not a document of Title.

1.2.11 FOB

Free on Board (FOB) means that all expenses till the goods cross the rails of the ship should be borne by the seller and any other expense should be borne by the buyer.

1.2.12 C&F

Cost and Freight (C&F) means that the price not only includes cost but also freight upto the port of destination.

1.2.13 CIF

CIF is that price which includes Cost, Insurance and Freight.

1.2.14 FAS

In Free Alongside Ship (FAS), the cost incurred up to placing the goods in port by the side of ship is credited to the account of seller while cost of loading it to ship etc. is credited to the account of buyer.

1.2.15 EX QUAY

In Ex Quay, the price not only includes cost, insurance and freight but also includes the clearing expenses incurred for clearing the goods from buyer's port.

1.2.16 Ex QUAY Duty Paid

Here the price also includes customs duty to be paid by the buyer.

1.2.17 INCO Terms

INCO terms are international commercial terms defined by the International Chamber of Commerce, defining the meaning of various terms as given above. If the international purchase orders are subjected to INCO terms then it will lead to uniformity in interpretation of various commercial terms.

1.2.18 Counter Trade

There are three forms of counter trade namely:

Barter: In barter, goods are exchanged instead of paying in money.

Buyback: In buyback supplier of capital goods undertakes to buyback goods manufactured from the capital goods.

Switch: Switch means that the proceeds of exports will be credited to an escrow* account which can be used to buy any goods from the country of imports.

Counter trade is an inefficient form of international trade and it is resorted to by countries having acute Balance of Payment** problem.

1.2.19 Packing Credit

Packing credit is given for financing exports. It can be classified as *pre-shipment credit or post-shipment credit*. Packing credit is given against export order or Letter of Credit. Pre shipment credit is given for procuring material, manufacture of finished goods, while post shipment credit is given for financing receivables out of exports. They are extended for a maximum period of 180 days which can be further extended for 90 days at the discretion of the bank. Maximum interest rate charged is Prime Lending Rate – 2.5% for rupee packing credit and LIBOR[1] + 0.75% for Packing credit in foreign currency. Packing credit can be extended in rupee to those exporters who are capable of managing their exchange rate exposure and for those who are not capable of managing their foreign currency exposure, the same can be

* Please see Glossary for the definition of Escrow account.

** Full details of BOP are provided in Chapter 2.

[1] For details refer 1.2.20

extended in any one of the four foreign currency (US $, Pound Sterling, Euro, Japanese Yen). Packing credit can be liquidated only out of export proceeds. Packing credit is an answer to the local exporter's complaint that interest rate on export credit is high, thereby making their goods uncompetitive in export markets.

Packing credit is extended at any time and export receivables are not subject to Maximum Permissible Bank Finance (MPBF) requirements. Bank can be extremely flexible with regard to margins. Post shipment credit is given by the bank in the form of discounting of export bills.

1.2.20 LIBOR

LIBOR means London Inter Bank Offered Rate. London is the premiere financial centre in the world. London Inter Bank Offered Rate is a benchmark floating rate at which one bank is willing to lend to another bank in inter-bank market. It is available for various tenures. LIBOR being the premier financial rate, this rate is used as landmark rate in many lending transactions.

1.2.21 LIBID

London Inter Bank Bid Rate is the rate at which one bank is willing to pay another bank for its borrowings in the international market in London Inter Bank Market. It is again available for various tenures.

1.2.22 Prime Rate

Prime rate is the rate at which a bank is willing to lend for its top rated customer.

1.2.23 ECGC

Export Credit Guarantee Corporation is under the Ministry of Commerce which grants insurance cover for exporters against political risk and credit risk. These risks are not usually insured and it is given as a measure of incentive to the exporters. ECGC covers are issued, insisted compulsorily for extending packing credit by banks. Now ECGC has started extending new covers like LC discrepancy cover to facilitate exports.

1.2.24 Seller's Credit

Seller's credit is extended by the bank to the seller of the instrument against a sales transaction. This may be for a single transaction or as a line of credit.

1.2.25 Buyer's Credit

Here the bank extends credit to buyer instead of seller either as a single transaction or as a line of credit.

1.2.26 Forfaiting

Forfaiting is export factoring. In forfaiting export bills are accepted by importer as well as by his bankers. Acceptance of Export bill by importer's bank is known as *Avalising* and the bank accepted export bill of exchange is known as *aval*.

Such Avalised bills are discounted by Forfaiting agency on non-recourse basis and proceeds are credited to exporter's account. Non-recourse basis means that in the event of importer's or his bank's failure to make payment, the loss will be borne by the forfaiting agency and will not be recovered from exporter. In India EXIM bank offers forfaiting against medium term export receivables. But unlike in international markets, there are no deep secondary markets for these avalised bills in India.

1.2.27 Bill of Entry

Bill of Entry is a document filed by the importer for import of goods into India. There are various bills of entry like bill of entry for home consumption, in bond bill of entry, exchange control copy of bill of entry. Assessable value for levying customs duty is determined based on bill of entry. Bank will remit the proceeds only against Exchange control copy of Bill of Entry as per the value mentioned in it.

1.2.28 Basic Customs duty

It is the duty levied under section 12 of the Customs Act on landed cost that is CIF Value of the goods calculated at the exchange rate notified by the Central Government. If freight is more than 20% of the value of the goods excess is ignored. Similarly if no freight details are provided to customs, 20% of the value of goods is taken as freight. Insurance is included as actuals, if no insurance details are given 1.125% of the value of goods is taken as insurance. 1% of CIF value is added as landing charges.

1.2.29 Countervailing Duty

Countervailing Duty is levied at the rate at which excise duty is levied. If the goods are manufactured in India, it is levied at Cost + Basic Customs duty.

1.2.30 Safeguard Duty

Safeguard duty is levied under section 8B of the Customs Act to prevent injury to Domestic Industry through huge quantities being imported.

1.2.31 Anti Dumping Duty

After WTO regulations, countries are drastically reducing customs duty to integrate with rest of the world. Many countries dump goods at lesser cost. To prevent these countries from dumping, anti-dumping duty based on the findings by appropriate anti-dumping authorities can be levied.

1.2.32 Special Additional Duty

Special Additional Duty is levied to defer the wish of swadeshi lobby and it is levied at the rates of sales tax applicable for local goods on Landed cost + Countervailing Duty. It now stands abolished.

1.2.33 Transfer Pricing

Due to increasing integration of world economy and transactions between different branches of subsidiaries, transfer pricing is being increasingly resorted to avoid payment of taxes. To counter these, such transactions in which prices are not determined on arms length basis, price is determined based on Comparable Uncontrolled Price method (CUP), Resale method, Transaction Net Margin method (TNNM), and Profit Split method. Of late increasingly developing countries are tightening their tax regimes to prevent leakage of revenue due to transfer pricing.

1.2.34 Red Channel

It is a channel prescribed for passengers coming from abroad to our country who carry dutiable goods to declare the same and pass through.

1.2.35 Green Channel

Green Channel is the channel for those passengers who do not carry dutiable goods beyond permitted limits from any other country into India.

1.2.36 Documentary Bills

Documentary Bills are those bills which are accompanied by the document of Title for the goods like LR/RR etc. If a bill of exchange is not accompanied by document of Title to the goods it is called as *Clean Bill*.

1.2.37 Currency Declaration Form or CDF

Currency Declaration Form (CDF) is that form by virtue of which a person travelling to India declares his amount of foreign currency to customs. A person carrying with him/her more than US $ 10,000 must declare the same to the customs though the Currency Declaration Form. Similarly those resident Indians who are travelling abroad cannot carry more than Rs.1000 outside of India.

1.3 THEORIES EXPLAINING THE NEED FOR INTERNATIONAL TRADE

1.3.1 Theory of Absolute Advantage

Adam Smith propounded the "Theory of Absolute Advantage". In this theory, Labour was considered the only factor of production. For example one country has absolute advantage in producing computer chips and another country has absolute advantage in producing potato chips, both can increase their wealth by producing goods in which they have absolute advantage and trading. Absolute advantage theory assumes absence of transaction cost[1] and tariff barrier[2].

1.3.2 Theory of Comparative Advantage

David Ricardo expounded the "Theory of comparative advantage". Again labour was considered as the only factor of production. As per this theory even if a nation has absolute advantage over another nation in producing both computer chips and potato chips still they can produce goods where they have comparative advantage and trade in them to increase wealth.

1.3.3 Theory of Imitation

Posner propounded the "Theory of Imitation". According to this theory if new goods are produced in a country due to innovation, it takes some time for the other country to imitate the production of the same. During this time international trading in goods should take place.

1.3.4 Theory of Product Life Cycle

As per the product life cycle theory a product has various stages like introduction, growth, maturity, and decline. New product invention takes place predominantly in developed countries. By the time they reach their maturity stage, the scope for growth gets tapered off leading to exploration in other markets (like developing markets) which in turn leads to international trade.

1.3.5 Theory of Intra-Industry Trade

The fact that some foreign countries are situated closer to some states of our country lead to intra-industry trade. For instance: The transportation cost for transporting goods from say Bangladesh (which is a foreign country situated closer to the state of West Bengal) to West Bengal is far cheaper than transporting the same goods from say Tamil Nadu or Karnataka to West Bengal (Both are states of the same country) leading to intra-industry trade.

[1] Refer to Glossary for details

[2] Go to 1.4.1 for the definition.

1.3.6 Heckshire Ohlin Model

Heckshire Ohlin model says that countries rich in capital will engage in capital intensive industry labour-rich will engage in labour-intensive industry. Thus, the United States of America, which is capital-rich can produce and trade in capital-rich goods, while India, which is labour-rich can produce and trade in labour-rich goods. But there is not much empirical evidence supporting this theory. For example US, which is capital-intensive, exports many labour-intensive goods.

1.4 BARRIERS TO INTERNATIONAL TRADE

All the above theories suggest that the flow of international trade is free and depends only on economic benefits. But many a times there are barriers to International trade in the form of Tariff, Non-tariff and Trade Barriers.

1.4.1 Tariff Barrier

Tariff barrier is in the form of levying high customs duty on goods imported.

1.4.2 Non-tariff Barrier

Non-tariff Barrier is in the form of quotas in licensing. Restrictive agreements like Multi-Fiber agreements for textiles also constitute one form of the Non-tariff barrier which is called as Trade Barrier. Some time quality barriers like Phyto Sanitary restriction for food articles as well as complying with country's mandatory quality standards are treated as Non-tariff barriers. Apart from this, discriminatory customs valuation is also adopted as Non-tariff barrier. Developing countries now feel that the environmental standards and labour standards proposed unilaterally by developed countries constitute Non-tariff barriers.

1.4.3 Trade Barriers

Trade Barriers are formed by entering into bilateral agreement and giving Most Favoured Nation (MFN) status to import from certain countries. Apart from this, Free Trade Zone, Customs Union, Common Market, Economic Union, Monetary Union and Cartels which restrict free flow of International Trade also come under Trade Barrier.

Extreme form of trade barrier is Embargo.

1.4.3.1 Free Trade Zone

In Free Trade Zone, goods move in the member countries without any customs duty. But individual countries who are members of Free Trade Zone can decide the Tariff and other restrictions, which they can place on imports from other than members of Free Trade Zone. North American Free Trade Association (NAFTA), which has US, Canada and Mexico as members, are examples of Free Trade Zone.

1.4.3.2 Customs Union

In Customs Union the members are exempt from customs duty while a uniform customs duty is imposed by all members of the Union for goods imported from countries which are not members of the Union.

1.4.3.3 Common Market

In Common Market not only goods but also services and service providers can move freely among member countries without any permit.

1.4.3.4 Economic Union

In Economic Union there is free movement of goods, services as well as service providers. Also the member countries decide their Economic, Agricultural, Fiscal and Monetary policies in co-ordination with each other.

1.4.3.5 Monetary Union

In Monetary Union there is mandated inflation, fiscal deficit, interest rate and a common currency with common central bank for the entire union. As in the case of European Union. It is a great achievement for European Union that eleven countries involved in the union are successful in retaining their political sovereignty and single currency at the same time.

1.5 NEED FOR ERECTING TRADE BARRIERS

Trade Barriers are erected for various reasons such as:

1. Revenue collection through customs duty.
2. Protecting Infant Industry: For example India imposed very high tariff Barrier for protecting its infant Industry. This is cited as the

main reason for poor quality of Indian goods and lack of competitiveness in Indian industry.

3. To counter adverse Balance of Payment position: Till early 90's Indian strategy was to stress for import substitution to set right Balance of Payment deficit through high tariff and non tariff barriers. This led to illegal activities like smuggling and bred corruption.
4. To protect local employment: This was again cited by India as a justification for imposing high tariff and non-tariff barriers leading to inefficiency and low productivity of Indian labour.
5. For political reasons like UN embargo on Iraq.

1.6 NEED FOR CREATING INTERNATIONAL TRADE ORGANIZATIONS

International community, through creation of International Trade Organization whose members are GATT, WTO and UNCTAD has tried to facilitate free trade and avoid Tariff and Non-tariff Barriers.

1.6.1 GATT

General Agreement on Trade and Tariff (GATT) was constituted in 1947 to facilitate free trade. It wanted to give MFN status to all its members and acted as adjudicator of inter-country trade disputes to prevent unilateral retaliation. The main objectives behind GATT were to:

- Progressively reduce tariff rates,
- Extend Most Favoured Nation treatment to all members,
- Remove quantitative restrictions, and
- Free exchange control on current account transactions.

Several rounds of discussions were held during Geneva Round, Kennedy Round, Tokyo Round, and Uruguay Round. But since it was an adhoc arrangement, it did not take into consideration trade in services and intellectual properties.

1.6.2 WTO

World Trade Organisation was constituted in 1995. Unlike GATT, WTO is permanent in nature. Apart from Trade and Services, it also deals with Trade Related Aspects of Intellectual Property Rights (TRIPS) wherein issues regarding Copyright, Patent, Industrial design, Trademarks are dealt with. In Trade Related Aspects of Investment Management (TRIMS), discrimination against Foreign Investments in the form of restriction, discriminatory taxation, and expropriation without compensation are dealt with. Apart from this, restrictive practices like Multi-Fiber Agreement for textiles are brought within the aegis of WTO.

The various objectives of WTO include implementation, administration and operation of all multilateral trade disputes, administration and operation of all multilateral trade agreements, administration of rules governing settlement of trade disputes, trade policy review mechanism, providing a forum for discussion between countries.

Since the trade barriers are getting dismantled there is a tendency on the part of exporters to dump goods. Dumping means selling goods below the price at which they are sold in the country of export. To prevent this country of import can levy anti-dumping duty.

WTO is perceived to be partial to developed countries. Right from its rounds in Uruguay, Seattle up to Cancun, it is perceived that the rich countries adopt an arrogant attitude and impose their will on poor countries; especially countries from Africa are never consulted. So much so that WTO is given an acronym *World Take Over*. Developed countries deny market access to developing countries through environment and labour standards, which the developing countries perceive as non-tariff barrier. While the developed countries impose their views by getting Patent laws amended for product patent with extended protection period of 20 years, Amended Trade Mark laws (to include service marks) make developing countries adopt copyright act with protection for 50 years, making them give up quotas and reduce tariffs, and abolish investment barriers like dividend balancing, buyback, as well as impose phasing out of fiscal concessions like phasing out of chapter VI under Indian Income Tax Act, but extend very little concessions as agreed in Uruguay Round such as reduction of Agricultural subsidies, Muti-Fibre arrangement for textiles, stricter Phytosanitary norms for food articles etc.

Cancun failure of WTO meet is a clear pointer that WTO mechanism will breakdown unless the consultative process is widened.

1.6.3 UNCTAD

United Nations Council for Trade and Development (UNCTAD) has been constituted to facilitate international trade. The first meeting was held in Geneva in 1964 and was attended by 120 countries. In 1964, it was made a permanent body by way of UN resolution. Its main aim was to reduce trade barriers in developed countries through increased access to their markets, improve the standard of living in developing countries. It also held conferences in New Delhi 1968 and SanDiego, Chile in 1972. Other than passing few resolutions, it hardly achieved anything. Even the objective of increasing the aid given by developed countries to developing countries for 0.7% of their GNP to 1.4% was never achieved. Since its incorporation but for achieving Generalized System of Preference (GSP) for imports from developing country to developed country, it has achieved very little. In spite of such efforts, freeing International trade from barriers has a long way to go.

1.7 SOME MORE TERMS USED IN INTERNATIONAL FINANCE

1.7.1 Exchange Control

Exchange Control means that the central bank of the country monitors foreign exchange and it is not possible to exchange the local currency for foreign currency and the local residents are prohibited from owning foreign currency.

1.7.2 Authorised Dealer

Authorised dealers are authorized by RBI to deal in foreign exchange and apart from buying and selling foreign currency, they can open foreign currency account abroad, open LCs, and remit foreign exchange abroad. Usually banks are the authorized dealers.

1.7.3 Money Changers

Money Changers can buy and sell foreign exchange including Traveller's cheques. But they cannot open LC or a foreign currency account and cannot remit foreign exchange abroad.

1.7.4 Restricted Money Changer

Restricted Money Changers can buy foreign exchange but cannot sell the same. Only these categories are authorized by RBI to deal in foreign exchange.

1.7.5 FEDAI

Foreign Exchange Dealers Association of India is an association of Authorised dealers which is a self-regulating agency through which RBI controls foreign exchange market.

1.7.6 Cash & Deferred Payment

Exports and Imports should be paid within 180 days of the date of shipment and these are called as cash payment terms and if imports are to be paid after 180 days from the date of shipment and export proceeds to be received after180 days from the date of shipment, then it is called as deferred payment terms which requires approval from RBI.

1.7.7 GR Form

Guaranteed Receipt Form or GR form is used by RBI for physical export to ascertain the value of export goods as well as to monitor their realization. It is prepared in duplicate and submitted to customs at the time of exports. Customs verify the value with contract and certify the same and one copy is given back to the exporter and other copy is sent by customs directly to RBI. Exporter has to forward this copy to authorized dealer with invoice etc. and the authorized dealer verifies the same with invoice value. He also monitors that exporter realizes the same within 180 days from the date of shipment in the case of cash payment term.

1.7.8 SDF

Special Declaration Facility or SDF performs the same function as that of GR form but the export is done through custom houses which are computerized in the form of Electronic Data Interchange (EDI).

1.7.9 PP Form

PP[3] form performs the same function as GR form, if the export is done through post. Authorised dealer instead of customs certify the PP form.

1.7.10 Softex Form

Softex Form performs the same function as that of GR form for software exports. Softex form value is verified and certified by Software Technology Park of India (STPI) under the Department of Electronics instead of customs.

1.7.11 ETX Form

In the case of cash payment if payment is not received within 180 days from the date of shipment, exporter has to file ETX[4] form explaining the reason for delay and needs to take approval from authorized dealers.

1.7.12 Shipping Bill

Like Bill of Entry being document for imports, Shipping Bill is a document of exports. There are various types of Shipping Bills such as: Free Shipping Bill, DEEC Shipping Bill or White Shipping Bill Export (for items which involve payment of duty) or Yellow Shipping Bill, Drawback Shipping Bill or Green Shipping Bill, DEPB Shipping bill or Blue Shipping Bill, and DFRC Shipping Bill. Customs certifies the Shipping Bill by recording the export order in the shipping bill. Based on the same export incentive can be claimed.

1.7.13 Capital Flight

FERA holds strict punishment for illegal movement of capital out of the country, but in spite of that capital goes out of the country through Hawala, Under Invoicing, Over Invoicing etc. and this is termed as Capital Flight.

---

[3] See Glossary for details.

[4] Refer to Glossary.

1.7.13.1 Hawala

As already mentioned foreign exchange can be operated only through authorised dealers, money changers and restricted money changers licensed by RBI. But a parallel illegal market operates in which supplier of foreign exchange are terrorists, drug peddlers. The rupee in this case is supplied by those people who earn it by carrying out illegal businesses like smuggling, corruption etc.

1.7.13.2 Under Invoicing

Exports are under invoiced which means the value invoiced is less than the value of the goods exported and the difference is remitted abroad to the secret account.

1.7.13.3 Over Invoicing

Imports are invoiced at a value more than the value of goods and difference is remitted to the foreign secret account.

In spite of threatening with punishment capital flight takes place through the above mentioned routes and the Government has now realized that the best way to attract and retain capital in India is not through legislation but by providing congenial atmosphere for investment in the form of reasonable level of taxes, clean administration, good infrastructure in the form of power, ports, telecommunication etc. Thus, keeping with the liberal thinking FEMA, which has much more trust has been enacted.

1.7.14 EEFC Account

Exchange Earners Foreign Currency Account is a facility given to exporters to keep part of their foreign currency earning in the form of foreign currency. Ordinary exporters can keep 30% foreign currency earned in EEFC account as current account without any interest payment. EOUs[5], Status holders and SEZ[6] can keep 100% of foreign exchange earned in EEFC Account. EEFC account can be used for any

[5] For details go to 1.10.5.

[6] For details go to 1.10.6.

purpose more liberally like for foreign investments, travel etc. without quantitative restrictions.

1.7.15 FOREIGN CURRENCY NON-RESIDENT (FCNR)

FCNR accounts are opened in one of the four specified foreign currencies US $, Pound Sterling, Euro and Japanese Yen. Both principal and interest are repatriable. Since the deposits are in foreign currency, the depositors are not subjected to exchange rate fluctuations.

Till early 90's FCNR (A) deposit could be opened where banks had to surrender foreign exchange to RBI at notional exchange rate and in turn the banks could get it back from RBI at the same notional rate. But now FCNR (B) can be opened where the banks need not surrender foreign exchange to RBI and can freely use the same. Banks lend it to corporates for a period of 6 months at Libor + 200 to 300 based points above the Libor.

1.7.16 NRE Account

Non-Resident External Account deposits or NRE account is kept in Indian rupee and both principle and interest are repatriable. In this account, depositor bears the exchange rate risk.

1.7.17 NRNR Account

In an NRNR account, depositor keeps the money in Indian rupee. The interest on the money is repatriable while the principle is not.

1.7.18 NRO Account

Non-Resident Ordinary Account or NRO account is kept in rupee and both principle and interest are not repatriable.

1.7.19 RFC

RBI can permit residents to open and maintain foreign currency account. These deposits were permitted for Indian citizens or persons of Indian origin. But in view of the comfortable foreign exchange reserve position, arbitrage opportunities are reduced by RBI by not bearing exchange risk and also reducing interest rates on these deposits.

1.8 DIFFERENCE BETWEEN FERA AND FEMA

Foreign exchange Regulation act (FERA) enacted in 1973 was replaced by Foreign Exchange Management Act (FEMA) in the year 2000 as per the liberalized philosophy of the government.

1. FERA regulates while FEMA facilitates as mentioned in preamble to the act.
2. FERA is prosecution oriented while FEMA remedy is civil in nature.
3. FERA defines residence based on intention, while FEMA residence is based on number of days of stay in India and is in alignment with Income Tax Act.
4. FERA does not define service exports while FEMA defines service exports.
5. FERA does not clearly define what are permitted transactions thereby everything has to be referred to RBI for approval while FEMA clearly specifies transactions which are prohibited, transactions which require prior approval of Central Bank, transactions which can be undertaken without any approval.
6. Even capital account transaction which requires prior approval of RBI as per FEMA, clear cut guidelines are laid out, which if followed would make approval automatic.
7. In FERA if the contract provides 30 days as credit period then 31st day itself is treated as overdue and the exporter has to take permission from RBI for extension, while in FEMA till 180 days from shipment the same is not treated as overdue irrespective of credit term in contract.

1.9 CAPITAL ACCOUNT CONVERTIBILITY*

Foreign Exchange Management Act (FEMA) does not permit capital account convertibility and there are two schools of thought whether India should go for capital account convertibility or not.

* For details refer Chapter 2 (Balance of Payments).

Those who argue for capital account convertibility plead that in these days of information technology revolution and internet banking and international credit card, placing restriction on capital movement is not feasible. Apart from this, if the new thinking is global integration money alone cannot stand apart. If rupee is made fully convertible then foreign investment will freely flow into the country.

But the school which argues against capital account convertibility believes that the time is not yet ripe for capital account convertibility. In a market dominated by speculators India with its miniscule reserves cannot take on a speculative attack on rupee. In support of this, they point out 1997 South East Asian crisis in which rupee escaped the contagion effect only due to capital account control. They support their argument with the opinion given by Mr. Paul Krugman, Nobel laureate from US, who supports exchange restriction in capital account for developing countries. This school of thought argues that once the country achieves mandated inflation, mandated fiscal deficit, adequate supervision for financial system, NPA (Non-Performing Assets) of banking system falling below mandated level, then capital account convertibility can be undertaken.

But what one has to take into account is the lack of governance and crony capitalism which are the main sources of crisis in addition to weak financial supervision rather than flow of hot money itself. In fact, it is the crisis which exposed the weakness in these tiger economies. Best solution is not to resist the international forces of integration, but to facilitate the same and to strengthen the domestic financial system to withstand any adverse effect of the same. Contagion cannot be controlled through exchange control because alternate illegal methods like hawala will be instituted to overcome the restrictions.

Of late signs are emanating from Government regarding free convertibility regime. Increasing liberalization (as suggested by increase in limits for advance remittance without Bank Guarantee, proof of imports limits enhancement, ECGC clearance being accepted as foreign exchange under FEMA, putting issue of ADR and GDR under automatic routes, permitting ADR and GDR issue to be retained abroad for takeover of foreign companies by Indian company, enhancing limit of overseas investment to $50 million per year, introducing rupee based options and derivatives like interest rate swap and Forward Rate agreements, allowing FDI without FIPB approval, permitting foreign companies to raise Indian depository receipt) is precursor to steady movement towards full convertibility regime.

As a prelude to full convertibility, there are several signs like free import of gold, increasing risk management like capital adequacy, ALM etc.

1.10 EXPORT IMPORT POLICY

Export Import policy is administered through Director General of Foreign Trade who is an official under Ministry of Commerce. Previously, the policy was called as Import Export policy and the focus was on controlling imports through licensing. From mid eighties, Government of India realized the importance of promoting exports. From 1992 the policy was rechristened as Export Import policy and more emphasis was placed on export promotion. It was converted to five year policy instead of annual policy to impart stability.

The following are the benefits given under export import policy for exporters.

1.10.1 Preshipment Benefits

Material can be imported in advance against export order, without the payment of duty, for use in exports through advance license. Only condition imposed is positive value addition.

Capital goods can be imported by paying 5% customs duty instead of normal duty by undertaking export obligation to be fulfilled over a period of eight years. Export obligation is linked to customs duty saved instead of the value of capital equipment. Even second hand capital goods are permitted to be imported under Export Promotion Capital Goods (EPCG) scheme.

1.10.2 Post Shipment Benefits

Post shipment benefits are given in the form of Duty Free Replenishment Certificate (DFRC), Duty Entitlement Passbook Scheme (DEPB) on completion of exports and realization of export proceeds. Post export benefits are given for those items for which Standard Input Output Norm (SION) is notified.

1.10.3 DFRC

After export and realization of sale proceeds Duty Free Replenishment Certificate DFRC is given for those materials which are allowed to be imported against the export of products as per SION. It can be either used by the exporter himself or sold in the market and premium realized. It is subject to minimum value addition requirements.

1.10.4 DEPB

Duty Entitlement Passbook Scheme DEPB is issued on post export and realization of export proceeds to products which are notified. Rates of DEPB are notified based on customs duty payable on products which can be imported as per SION for products which are exported. It operates as passbook scheme of bank. Any item can be imported against duty credit instead of specified items as in the case of DFRC. Thus, it is more flexible and valuable.

1.10.5 Deemed Exports

These are supplies made in India which are deemed as exports since they are made under internationally competitive conditions and involve savings in foreign exchange. Supplies to projects financed by World Bank, where contracts are awarded by way of global or limited tender, supply to power projects or fertilizer projects for equipment can be imported duty free. Supply to EOU, SEZ are treated as deemed exports under export import policy and commerce ministry provides concessions like, refund of terminal excise duty, intermediary advance license, duty drawback, DFRC etc. Finance Ministry does not recognize the concept of deemed export since the goods do not leave the shores of the country. It requires lot of educational efforts to popularize this important concept of foreign exchange savings.

1.10.6 EXPORT ORIENTED UNIT (EOU)

EOU can be set up in any place which is notified as warehousing station by Chief Commissioner of Customs. There are at present 300 such warehousing stations notified throughout India. EOUs at present operate under customs bond and customs supervision. They cannot do trading. They can sell up to 50% of FOB value of exports in domestic market by paying 50% customs duty applicable for import of product or excise duty whichever is more. Even 100% foreign equity can be held for items reserved for manufacture by small scale sector. They are expected to earn only positive Net Foreign Exchange (NFE). They can import all capital goods including second hand capital goods as well as raw material, components, consumables and packing materials without payment of customs duty. They can procure indigenous capital goods, raw material, components, packing material and consumables without payment of excise duty. Many State Governments have exempted sales tax for material procured by EOU. Development Commissioner who is the registering authority for EOU acts as a single window clearance agency for EOU. They are given green card to facilitate quick clearance by customs. EOU's consignments are inspected by customs at the premises of EOU and not at the port. They are also given income tax exemption.

1.10.7 SEZ

Special Economic Zones or SEZ is a concept borrowed from China. These zones are treated as foreign country within the country and are subjected to minimum restrictions. They have to be located in notified place like Hassan in Karnataka, Nanguneri or Kakinada in Andhra Pradesh etc. They are only subjected to minimum NFE conditions. 100% foreign equity is permitted other than for trading. Domestic sales can be made by paying customs duty equivalent for similar goods imported.

In addition to these concessions, the government should realize that export promotion should be defined in relative terms. If we have to compete with countries like China then infrastructure should improve, tariff barriers should be reduced to international level, the mindset of Indian industry should be made more outward-oriented.

1.10.8 Duty Drawback

Customs duty paid on input material used for export production and excise duty paid, for which Cenvat credit[7] is not availed, can be reimbursed through Duty Drawback which is provided under section 75 of the Customs Act. Based on statistics provided by trade associations, Government of India periodically notifies rates for various products which are termed as All Industry Rate. Based on the same concept, Duty Drawback can be claimed by the exporter without any further proof. But if the products exported by the exporter are not covered by All Industry Rates the exporter can prepare application for fixation of brand rate by filling up forms DBK I, DBK II & DBK III and get the rates fixed by Jurisdictional Central Excise Commissioner. Even if All Industry Rate is

[7] Go to glossary for details.

specified and if the rate fixed is less than 80% of what is actually to be reimbursed to the exporter, he can apply for special brand rates in DBK I, II & III. The Central Excise Commissioner will verify the rate submitted by exporter and issue rate letter confirming the percentage of reimbursement. When the items are exported under claim for drawback, they should be exported under drawback shipping bill. Based on the brand letter refund can be obtained from customs for Drawback. Banks give advance payment pending reimbursement of Drawback claim.

1.11 FOREIGN INVESTMENT

There are two types of Foreign Investments.

- Foreign Direct Investment
- Portfolio Investment.

An investor who wants to do portfolio investment or FDI has to assess the country risk involving natural resources, availability of educated manpower, attitude of the country to the foreign capital, risk of discriminatory taxes, nationalization or expropriation, blocking remittance, infrastructure, stability of the Government, independence of legal system and its quality, infrastructure in the form of roads, ports, housing, power, and water. The unique advantage of the country in the sector in which the investor proposes to invest is the disparity in income and existence of large middle class. If the investor finds that it is not possible to do research on individual company, he can invest through mutual funds.

1.11.1 Foreign Direct Investment

Foreign Direct investment involves equity participation in new ventures by foreigners.

1.11.2 Portfolio Management

Portfolio Management involves investment in the stock market. It cannot be argued that FDI is good and portfolio investment is not good. Primary and secondary market has got linkages and secondary market becomes liquid due to portfolio investment. This market automatically has a spill over effect and improves primary market. In fact, foreign capital in secondary market brings in best practices as experienced in Indian market like screen based trading, demat facilities, introduction of derivatives etc.

1.12 WHY DOES FOREIGN INVESTMENT TAKE PLACE?

Foreign markets and domestic markets are segmented due to restriction in convertibility of certain currencies, different business cycles in economy of different countries, investor's habit of investing only in domestic market, lack of information etc.

Due to these factors, the correlation coefficient between these markets is not equal to one. Therefore, Markowitz Theory of Portfolio Management is applicable when the efficiency frontier can be increased by diversifying investment into these markets whereby for the same risk more return can be earned or for same return risk level can be lowered.

But foreign investments are subjected to country or political risk, whereby the political authority of the country where the investment is made may impose restriction on repatriation, nationalize with compensation or expropriate without compensation. These investments are also subject to risk of adverse movements in exchange rate. If these risks are positively correlated they can get compounded further.

Political risk can be managed by investing in debt instrument rather than equity. In the event of exchange restrictions usually payment of interest and repayment of principle for debt is not restricted.

Apart from this, nearness to raw material, following the customers, protecting the brand equity, secrecy of technology, adverse exchange rate movements, scaling tariff barriers are few other reasons for FDI. Some examples of these factors are given below:

1. *Nearness to Raw material:* For example a cement manufacturer would like to be near the source of raw material like limestone.
2. *Following the Customer*: Big audit firms set up office internationally whenever their customers move to these countries.
3. *Protecting the Brand Equity:* For example MacDonald's wants to protect its brand equity by establishing its presence throughout the world rather than taking franchising route.
4. *Secrecy of Technology:* For example Coke's formula for manufacture is a secret so that it has to set up its own plant to manufacture Coke throughout the world rather than through the route of selling technology or through foreign collaboration.
5. *Adverse Exchange Rate Movement:* When a country's exchange rate appreciates then the cost of the country's product increases thereby

adversely affecting its competitive position, forcing it to move to other countries. As it happened in 80's when Japan moved its production base to other South East Asian Nations like South Korea, Taiwan leading to the emergence of Tiger economies in South East Asia.

6. *Scaling Tariff Barrier:* Sometimes countries move their manufacturing base to other countries to scale high tariff barrier.

7. *Due to product life cycle:* When an item reaches maturity stage in developed market it moves to developing market in search of growth leading to FDI. In developing countries savings are low because income is low; since savings are low investment is low; and because investment is low income is low. To break this vicious cycle of poverty foreign capital is required. In addition to this, due to institutional underdevelopment, means of financing infrastructure, so crucial for development, are not available and here the foreign capital can provide necessary impetus. Apart from this, foreign equity investment is accompanied by technology transfer, which is crucial for development. Foreign capital market brings with it best practices in terms of improved stock market practices, accounting standards and disclosure requirements. Usually developing countries run current account deficit and balance the same through capital account surplus in the form of FDI.

Attracting hot money is dangerous as evidenced by South East Asian experience, where the economies lost their Tiger status due to speculators withdrawing their money owing to adverse economic climate.

Today, India has made foreign investment almost free but for sectors such as: Atomic Energy, and Defense. For items reserved for production by small scale industries, a cap on foreign investment is kept. But even this is not applicable for EOU. The old ideological moorings like "yes" to computer chips and "no" to potato chips have gone, but there are irritants like "No Objection Certificate" from existing promoters, if the partner of joint venture wants to start a new unit.

As already proved by Chinese market, access and investment rather than aid ensures development.

1.13 EXAMPLES

1. An American investor purchased securities in Indian market by investing one million dollars, at the time of investing exchange rate is 50/50.5 Rs while one year latter the exchange rate is 53/54 Rs. What is the rate of return to American Investor if the rate of rupee return on Indian security is 20%, 25% & 50%

   If the rate is 20%

   Amount invested in India 10,00,000* 50= 5,0000000

   Return = 1,00,00,000

   After one year the amount to be repatriated = 60000000/54

   = 11,11,111

   Thus rate of return is = 1.11,111/ 10,00,000= 11.11%

   If the rate is 25%

   Amount invested is 10,00,000* 50= 5,00,000,00

   At 25% return rate of return in Indian rupee = 5,00,000,00* .25

   = 1,25,00,000

   At the closing rate = 6,25,00,000/54= 1157407

   Return = 157407/ 10,00,000= 15.74%

   If the rate is 50% in Indian Rupee term

   Investment = 5,00,000,00

   Return in Indian Rupee = 5,00,000,00*.50

   = 2,50,00,000 Rs

   Total amount to be repatriated in Rupees = 7,50,00,000/ 54

   = 13,88,889 $

   Return on investment= 3,88,889/ 10,00,000

   = 38.89%

2. Risk free return in India is 8%, an American Investor wants to invest in Indian securities with beta of 2, with variance of 15%, while exchange rate of rupee depreciates by 10% with variance of 20%. Market related return is 18% and correlation coefficient between return on security and exchange rate is 25%, find out the expected rate of return and risk in investments.

As per CAPM the expected return on security = Risk free interest rate + beta (market rate- risk free interest rate)

= .08 + 2(.18-.08)

= 28%

If 100 $ are invested in market then return is 128$, then excluding exchange rate

128* .9 – 100/ 100= 15.2%

Variance of return = .15+ .20 + 2* .25 square root of (.15* .20)

= .35 +. /09

= 44% risk.

CONCLUSION

In this chapter we discussed about the need for globalization due to integration of world market. Also various theories for indulging in International Finance like theory of absolute advantage, comparative advantage, Heckshire Ohlin Model, Posner model of imitation, product lifecycle model; various types of LCs like revocable, irrevocable, confirmed letter of credit, red clause and green clause letter of credit and various terms of trade like FOB, FAS, C&F, CIF , EX Quay etc., terms like LIBOR, LIBID, Packing credit, exchange control, capital account convertibility, EEFC, Open credit, FDI, WTO were discussed in detail.

SUGGESTED ASSIGNMENTS

1. Critically examine the function which has facilitated globalization of Financial Market.
2. What is meant by Packing Credit?
3. What is a Documentary Bill?
4. What are the credits available for Indian exporter to finance his exports?
5. Distinguish between DA and DP mode of payment?
6. What is meant by confirmed Letter of Credit?
7. Mention any three objectives of WTO agreements.
8. Mention any three objectives of WTO agreements. What is meant by capital flight?
9. Explain the need and significance of capital account convertibility?
10. What is meant by Exchange Earners Foreign Currency Account?
11. Critically examine the need for and significance of Capital Account Convertibility
12. What are the motives for FDI?

Chapter 2

Balance of Payment

2.1 INTRODUCTION

Balance of Payment position emerges due to the trading between residents of the country with the rest of the world. Balance of Trade position is due to trading in physical goods only. It is considered positive if the export of goods is more than the import of goods. In Balance of Payment not only goods but also export and import of services are considered as in Current Account Transaction apart from trading in goods and services, transfers like gift, grant, transfer of residence, and pension payment for past services are considered.

In Capital Account Transaction all assets held by the foreigner in the home country including bank deposits lead to *Capital Account Surplus* while all assets held by resident in the foreign country are considered as *Capital Account Deficit*. The composition of the official reserves of a country can be studied only by studying Balance of Trade, Balance of Payment as well as Capital and Current Account. If the Balance of payment is negative it means that the domestic consumption is more than domestic savings which in turn means that the country is living beyond its means and therefore there is a demand for foreign currency which will lead to appreciation of foreign currency and depreciation of domestic currency. If there is surplus in balance of payment then it means that the country is living below its means thereby domestic currency will appreciate and foreign currency will depreciate. In addition to this, if there is a structural problem in the Balance of Payment, the country has to actively scout for foreign capital and has to liberalize thereby leading to increased competition in domestic market. If there is surplus in Balance of Payment, increased investments abroad will be allowed.

Balance of Payment statistics are important for a finance manager, since it will indicate the direction of movement of exchange rates. For example if the Balance of Payment is negative then it means that the demand for foreign currency is more and it will appreciate. If the Balance of Payment is positive it means that the demand for domestic currency is more indicating that it can appreciate.

Balance of Payment can be indicated by way of the following equation:

$$Y = C+G+I+X-M$$

Where Y is National Income, C is Consumption, G is Government Expenditure, I is Investment, X is exports, M is Imports.

$$X-M = Y-(C+G+I)$$

Y can also be expressed by way of equation

$$Y = C+T+S$$

Where T is taxes, S is savings.

Substituting Y

$$X-M = C+T+S-(C+G+I)$$

$$= T-G+(S-I)$$

Thus, negative Balance of Payments can be corrected by increasing taxes, reducing government expenditure - in other words reducing fiscal deficit - by increasing savings and by reducing consumption.

Balance of Payment disequilibrium can be remedied by borrowing from international institutions like IMF which is called as *Multilateral Borrowings* or by inter-governmental borrowing called as *Bilateral Borrowing* thus, encouraging Foreign Direct Investment or Portfolio Investment, deflating the domestic economy, and devaluing the domestic currency. Other than this, exchange control can also be considered as a direct option for remedying the BOP position.

Balance of Payment transactions can be classified as *autonomous transactions* as well as *accommodating transactions*. Autonomous transaction takes place due to import and export of goods and services.

Accommodating transaction means borrowing to rectify Current Account Deficit. It is said that a developing country instead of living below its means and in poverty can run Current Account Deficit and borrow to invest.

In India, Balance of Payment is dependent on price of crude. If international crude price firms up we can see that the Indian Balance of Payment decreases and RBI increases interest rates thereby abandoning soft interest rate regime to prevent exchange rate depreciation.

Balance of Payment is mostly negative for developing countries. This is due to the adverse terms of trade for them. Till recently, developing countries were exporting primary commodities whose price was declining, while the price of imported manufactured goods which they were importing was increasing. Of late, revival of service exports has given hope to countries like India. Software exports bring in huge amount of foreign exchange. India with its huge reserves of educated English speaking manpower tends to become the back office of the world hence promising to rake in more foreign exchange. Even in export of goods, the commodities are becoming more diversified, instead of gems, jewellery, diamonds, pepper and cardamom the basket is diversifying to engineering, chemicals and other manufactured goods.

IMF manual wants imports and exports to be measured at the time of transaction at the exchange rate prevailing on the date of transaction. But in case of India, the exports are accounted at the time of exports at FOB value, while imports are accounted at the time of payment at CIF value at average exchange rates. Service payments like interest and dividends are accounted at the time of payment instead of at the time of accrual.

Today India is realizing the potential of services and is actively encouraging software exports and other services like call centres through fiscal incentives and through setting up single window clearance like STPI.

2.2 RECORDING THE BALANCE OF PAYMENT

Balance of payment can be recorded by way of double entry. For example for export of goods on DA terms, the entry will be

Due from the Foreigner Dr

Export of Merchandise Cr

Similarly for service exports against acceptance of DA bill, entry will be

Due from Foreigner Dr

Trade in Services Cr

If the Bill of exchange is liquidated by the foreign party and amount is kept in foreign deposit, the entry will be

Foreign Asset Dr

Due from Foreigner Cr

When the foreign exchange is sold to Indian bank, no entry is required since one form of foreign exchange asset is converted to other form.

When foreign exchange is ultimately sold to Central bank, entry will be

Foreign Exchange Reserve a/c Dr

Foreign Exchange Asset Cr

When remittance is made by way of gift by foreigner to India, entry will be

Foreign Exchange Asset Dr

Unrequited Transfer Cr

When the Indian Bank sells this foreign currency to RBI, entry will be

Foreign Exchange Reserve Dr

Foreign Exchange Asset Cr

When Foreign Direct Investment is received, entry will be

Foreign Exchange Asset Dr

Foreign Direct Investment Cr

When this foreign exchange is sold by Indian bank to RBI, entry will be

Foreign Currency Reserve e.g. Dr

Foreign Exchange Asset e.g. Cr

When dividend or interest is paid on foreign investment or loan, entry will be

Trade in Services Dr

Foreign Exchange Asset Cr

When the Indian bank draws foreign currency from RBI, entry will be

Foreign Exchange Asset Dr

Foreign Exchange Reserves Cr

When remittance like gifts is made by Indian resident to foreigner, entry will be

Unrequited Remittance Dr

Foreign Exchange Asset Cr

If the Indian Bank draws foreign exchange from RBI, the entry will be

Foreign Exchange Asset Dr

Foreign Current Reserves Cr

If the imports are made on credit terms to a foreigner, then the entry will be

Merchandise Imports Dr

Liability to Foreigner Cr

If bank remits the amount to foreigner, entry will be

Liability to Foreigner Dr

Foreign Currency Asset Cr

If the Indian bank draws foreign exchange from RBI, entry will be

Foreign Currency Asset Dr

Foreign Currency Reserves Cr

If a person transfers his residence from abroad to India, entry will be

Foreign Currency Asset Dr

Unrequited Remittance Cr

If the bank transfers foreign currency to RBI, entry will be

Foreign Currency Reserve Dr

Foreign Currency Asset Cr

Inter-governmental borrowings and IMF credits are directly accounted in foreign exchange reserves.

Borrowing from IMF in SDR, entry will be

Official Reserves Dr

IMF Borrowing in SDR Cr

Thus, it can be seen that all Balance of Payment transactions are accounted as double entry, hence there can be no imbalance from an accountant's sense.

The Balance of Payment transactions can be classified as *above the line* and *below the line* transaction like in the case of Profit and Loss (P&L) accounts.

All above the line transactions take place autonomously and they are called as autonomous transactions as in the case of import and export of goods and services. All below the line transactions are called as accommodating transactions as in the case of FDI and loan.

It is considered better from the developing countries perspective to run a Current Account Deficit and finance the same through FDI.

CONCLUSION

Balance of Payment statistics are important for a Finance Manager since it determines the demand and supply of the currency, Government expenditure, taxes, private consumption, Investment etc. BOP can be classified as current account and capital account. A current account deficit means that one lives beyond his means while a current account surplus means living below his means. For a developing country current account deficit bridged through FDI is considered appropriate.

SUGGESTED ASSIGNMENTS

1. Why should a corporate finance manager monitor Balance of Payment developments?
2. Worked out example:

   Make the following entries and prepare current account, capital account and reserves.

1. Export of goods against Bills of exchange Rs. 15,000.
2. Realization of Bills of exchange and deposit in foreign bank account.
3. Sale of foreign exchange to domestic bank.
4. Sale of currency to RBI.
5. Export of software services Rs. 20,000 for cash.
6. Sale of foreign exchange by Bank to RBI.

7. Remittance for medical services availed abroad Rs. 25,000
8. Import on credit Rs. 30,000.
9. Remittance of foreign currency.
10. IMF credit in SDR Rs. 50,000.
11. Foreign investment Rs. 40,000
12. Remittance of dividend Rs. 5,000

Solution

1.	Due from Foreigner	Dr 15,000
	Export of Merchandise	Cr 15,000
2.	Foreign Assets	Dr 15,000
	Due from Foreigner	Cr 15,000
3.	No entry	
4.	Foreign Exchange Reserve	Dr 15,000
	Foreign Assets	Cr 15,000
5.	Foreign Assets	Dr 20,000
	Trade in Services	Cr 20,000
6.	Foreign Exchange Reserve	Dr 20,000
	Foreign Exchange Assets	Cr 20,000
7.	Foreign Assets	Cr 25,000
	Trade in Services	Dr 25,000
	Foreign Exchange Reserve	Cr 25,000
	Foreign Exchange Assets	Dr 25,000
8.	Merchandise Imports	Dr 30,000
	Liability to Foreigner	Cr 30,000
9.	Liability to Foreigner	Dr 30,000
	Foreign Exchange Assets	Cr 30,000
	Foreign Exchange Asset	Dr 30,000
	Foreign Exchange Reserve	Cr 30,000
10.	Foreign Exchange Reserve	Dr 50,000
	IMF SDR Loan	Cr 50,000
11.	Foreign Exchange Assets	Dr 40,000

FDI	Cr 40,000
Foreign Exchange Reserve	Dr 40,000
Foreign Exchange Asset	Cr 40,000
12. Sevices Dividend	Dr 5,000
Foreign Exchange Asset	Cr 5,000
Foreign Exchange Asset	Dr 5,000
Foreign Exchange Reserve	Cr 5,000
Current Account	
Merchandise Export	Cr 15,000
Trade in Services	Cr 20,000
Trade in Services	Dr 25,000
Merchandise Imports	Dr 30,000
Dividend	Dr 5,000
Current Account Balance	Dr 25,000
Capital Account	
IMF SDR Loan	Cr 50,000
FDI	Cr 40,000
Credit Balance	Rs. 90,000
Foreign Exchange Reserve	
Export Merchandise	Dr 15,000
Export Services	Dr 20,000
Medical expenses	Cr 25,000
Merchandise imports	Cr 30,000
Dividend	Cr 5,000
IMF SDR loan	Dr 50,000
FDI	Dr 40,000
Net Balance debit	Dr 65,000

Chapter 3

International Monetary System

3.1 INTRODUCTION

Initially there was gold standard system which started in 1814 in UK and 1870 in USA. In this system, each currency derived its value from its gold content. This led to the phenomenon of people taking the gold content in the currency whenever they felt that the gold content was more valuable than the currency value leading to Gresham's law which propounded that bad money replaces good money. Later Fiat Money that is paper money fully backed and exchangeable for gold was introduced.

Gold standard was replaced by Gold Exchange Standard wherein each country backed its currency by such currencies like US Dollar and Pound Sterling which were fully backed by Gold. Gold standard worked well in a pre-industrial society where the liquidity need was not that much and where it also acted as an effective check against countries printing money for the sake of political expediency leading to profligacy. But in a post-industrial society, restricting money supply based on the stock of gold rather than based on the needs of the real economy was not adequate. In fact, there are many economists who believe that the great depression of 1930s occurred due to inability of monetary sector to keep pace with real sector due to restriction imposed by Gold Exchange Standard.

After the arrival of great depression of 1930s, many countries thought that they can increase their share of international trade through devaluing their currencies which lead to retaliation from other countries resulting in what is popularly called as *Competitive Devaluation.* Countries also adopted multiple exchange rates leading to utter chaos in international financial market. It was felt that there was a need for controlling the currency movements to facilitate free flow of international trade.

In 1944, in a place called Bretten Wood, in New Hampshire USA, two institutions were created and they were called as Bretten Wood twins. These were World Bank and IMF.

3.1.1 World Bank

World Bank lends for international projects and it lends at a margin of half percent over its borrowing cost. International Development Agency (IDA) is the soft lending arm of World Bank. International Financial Corporation (IFC) lends to the private sector. The World Bank also provides technical assistance and advice to developing countries.

3.1.1.1 Asian Development Bank

Asian Development Bank was set up as an Asian version of World Bank to provide development finance to countries in Asian Region with headquarters in Manila, Phillipines.

3.1.1.2 IFC

International Finance Corporation or IFC is a member of World Bank group. It helps private sector projects in developing countries in the form of giving direct assistance, underwriting issues, undertaking feasibility studies for projects in private sector. It further acts as a guarantor for any lending to private sector and develops capital markets in these countries. Interest rate charged for these lendings being high risk in nature are quite high.

3.1.1.3 IDA

International Development Agency IDA is the soft lending arm of the World Bank, which finances predominantly development projects like drinking water projects, roads etc. They have very low or zero interest rates and long repayment schedule.

3.1.2 International Monetary Fund (IMF)

IMF was constituted to maintain exchange rate. Member countries were asked to contribute quota. Instead of each country exchanging gold for its currency, parity of gold was fixed in terms of US dollar. One ounce of gold was to be exchanged for 35$ by Federal Reserve which is the US Central bank. The parity of other currencies was fixed against US dollar based on the gold reserves. Fluctuation was allowed in this parity within a band of ± 1%.

Further devaluation required prior approval of IMF. IMF established contingency reserve to tide over temporary Balance of Payment difficulty, while Structural Reserve was established to tide over Structural Balance of Payment problems. Countries with chronic Balance of Payment deficits were allowed to depreciate their currencies.

IMF extends standby facility; extended fund facility is to cover Structural Balance of payment problems. Even though conditionalities imposed by IMF are understandable from lender's perspective, the unimaginative manner in which IMF imposes straitjacket and uniform conditionalities without considering each country's peculiarities has come in for lot of criticism.

Recognizing the need for the increase in aid from rich countries to increase international liquidity and market access, increase of aid will be the focus in future. At the same time developing countries, instead of criticizing IMF, should recognize that IMF is an important benefactor for developing countries and they should try to stabilize their exchange rates through prudent fiscal policy and better governance.

3.2 FIXED EXCHANGE RATE SYSTEM

International Monetary System is moving towards two systems, one is fixed rate system, other one is floating rate system. Even though Bretten Wood system of fixed exchange rate is dead and gone, fixed exchange rate is done through Dollarisation policy wherein dollar is adopted as local currency as in the case of Panama, Ecuador etc. The other fixed exchange rate policy is implemented through Currency Board System, where local currency issue is pegged to dollar reserves held as in the case of Hong Kong, Argentina.

In fact this rigid system is cited as the main reason for rise of German and Japanese economy whose currencies were never allowed to appreciate to the extent to which their exports went up. The basis of fixed exchange rate system was international confidence in Dollar and (Federal Reserve) Fed's ability to exchange gold for dollar.

In 1960s due to cold war with Soviet Union, US military spending increased. Also, Vietnam War led to the increase in military spending. This resulted in widening budget deficit in US. US printed Dollars to counter this situation and dollar being international currency, others acquired dollar as a reserve currency. Thus, by simply printing dollars, US was able to finance its budget deficit and this was termed as *Seignoring*. Seignoring resulted in lack of fiscal discipline in US. More the dollar was printed less was US Federal Reserve's ability to exchange dollar for gold and this paradox was called as *Triffin's Paradox* named after the professor of Yale University who discovered this paradox.

Because of Seignoring, countries started losing faith in dollar as a reserve currency. Increasingly countries started exchanging dollar for gold, spearheaded by France. In 1968 US unilaterally announced that it will exchange dollar for gold only against Central Bank Reserves. This was the first blow to the fixed exchange rate system.

In 1971 US unilaterally announced that it will not exchange dollar for gold whether held by Central banks or others. This announcement led to the dismantling of fixed exchange rate system. In the absence of gold, countries met in Smithsonian Institute to revive fixed exchange rate system without the backing of gold.

1973 oil shock led to the collapse of fixed exchange rate system and several countries started floating their currencies. Even now countries like Hong Kong follow Currency Board System which closely resembles fixed exchange rate system. In this system, printing of currency is linked to dollar reserve held by Central bank instead of gold. Countries like Ecuador have substituted dollar for their domestic currency and this policy is called as *Dollaraisation*. SDRs are called as Special Drawing Rights. They are not currencies which are traded but consist of basket of currencies, which a country can borrow by selling gold to tide over Balance of Payment crisis.

SDRs were introduced by IMF to tide over international liquidity crisis due to oil shock. SDRs can be drawn without any contribution by the members and once drawn these need not be paid back. SDRs are normally not used for purchasing goods but mainly used for acquiring other currencies. SDRs are primarily used as a vehicle for solving Balance of Payment problem and cannot be used to transfer resources from developed to developing countries. A country can exchange twice the value of its quota of its currency to SDR.

If devaluation of a currency is done due to inelasticity in demand and supply, the exports will decline first for some period before exports increase and imports will increase for some period before exports decrease. This phenomenon of worsening of Balance of Payment immediately after devaluation before improving is called J-curve effect and was given by Marshall Lerner. This curve resembles English letter 'J'. Today, various pegs like crawling peg, peg with band are used for fixed exchange rate system.

3.3 FLOATING RATE SYSTEM

Floating exchange rate as already mentioned is either a free float or managed float.

In floating rate system, the rate of exchange is determined by the forces of demand and supply. Currency being associated with political sovereignty, it is allowed to float within a band determined by the political authority and the Central bank of the country, this is termed as *Managed Float* and *Dirty Float*.

Managed float does not facilitate international trade. During eighties when Japan was running huge surpluses with US, the US Government accused Japanese Government of manipulating exchange and not allowing appreciation of Japanese Yen to the desired extent, thereby preventing correction in Balance of Payment. US threatened Japan with unilateral action.

To avoid this situation, countries realized that they should take coordinated action on exchange rates. Thus, G7 was constituted consisting of US, UK, France, Germany, Italy, Japan and Canada.

During 90s due to the introduction of information technology, speculators took over from fundamental forces. The first vestige of this was seen in George Soros attack on Pound Sterling. George Soros again attacked Spanish Peseta and Italian Lira. Money moved across the world at lightning speed in search of quick returns and that is why it was known as *hot money*. Speculators again demonstrated their powers in South East Asian crisis of 1997.

It is said that floating exchange rate, due to its fluctuating nature, destabilizes trade and leads to cost push inflation. But this argument is not acceptable since floating exchange rate adjusts on a continuous basis but fixed exchange rate does one off big adjustment which has an element of shock far higher than floating exchange rate system.

3.4 FOREIGN EXCHANGE MARKET

Foreign Exchange Market is a 24-hour market with various centers like New York, London, Frankfurt, Bahrain, Tokyo, and Singapore. With huge number of players and huge transactions, it becomes impossible for any single player to influence the market. Thus, it has truly become an efficient market. There are many essentials, which are required for making this market efficient. These are:

3.4.1 SWIFT

SWIFT is the Society for Worldwide InterBank Financial Telecommunication. It replaces paper by electronic fund transfer by secure SWIFT codes, thereby reducing transaction costs. It is supported by 1200 professional organizations throughout the world. Banks, Bond Holders, Investment Bankers, Brokers and finance companies are its main customers.

3.4.2 Reuters

Reuter is a London based organization established in the year 1851. First Electronic trading screen which gives real time quotes was established in the year 1973 by Reuters.

3.4.3 Telrate

Telrate is an American organization established in 1969 to deal in screen based trading for foreign exchange.

3.4.4 CHIPS

Clearing House for Interbank Payment System is a US based electronics payment system.

3.4.5 CHAPS

Clearing House for Automated Payment System is a UK based electronic payment System.

3.4.6 Euroclear

Euroclear is a Brussels based organization, involved in large scale bond clearance.

3.4.7 CEDEL

Cedel is in Luxembourg, involved in large scale bond clearance.

Efficient Market is a market involving huge transactions, with large number of players. Nobody can influence the market; information is perfect and past trend cannot be used to predict future market trend. There are various participants in foreign exchange markets; they are importers, exporters, Central banks, Hedgers, speculators and arbitrageurs, dealers in foreign exchange.

3.4.8 Hedging

Hedging means taking position in both spot and forward market.

3.4.9 Speculation

Speculation means taking position in forward market only and it is highly risky.

3.4.10 Arbitraguer

Arbitraging means making risk less profit by taking advantage of market imperfections. Foreign exchange market being an efficient market gives very little scope for arbitraging.

3.4.11 Changing Trends in Foreign Exchange Market

In future it is expected with electronic fund transfers and trading, dismantling of exchange control by many of the countries, regulatory authority for derivative trading especially over the counter derivatives, increasing disclosure of over the counter derivatives to make it more transparent to avoid situations like LTCM collapse, emergence of separate laws for derivatives since the existing laws are inadequate to regulate. Disappearance of smaller currencies and the emergence of fewer currencies in the international scenario is backed by emergence of the EURO. In future it is expected Dollar block, Yen block currencies and Euro would be three major traded currencies A centralized authority for regulating currency will emerge on the lines of WTO, a centralized authority for regulating international trade and European Central bank is a precursor to this trend. Apart from this, international integration through International disclosures, establishment of Basel norms for capital adequacy and corporate governance are pointing towards the trend of international integration. The role of Bretten Wood twins would be drastically redefined. Countries have to choose between any two of the three namely: sovereignty, globalization, and regulation. Hedge funds would be subjected to international regulations. Politically, world will integrate more and national boundaries will collapse.

3.5 EURO MARKET

Prime reason for development of Euro currency is political. In 1950s, due to the prevalence of cold war, Russia kept its dollar deposits with banks in London, Germany and France because of the fear that the US Government would freeze its deposits. Again, Organisation of Petroleum Exporting Countries (OPEC) countries kept their dollar deposits in London since they suspected that US favours Israel and would freeze their dollar deposits.

A virtue was found out in such deposits kept out of political necessity. Since these were kept outside the country of the currency, monetary authorities could not place any restrictions on the issue of such currencies like reserve requirements, withholding tax for foreign borrowers, compulsory credit rating for borrowers, deposit insurance etc. Apart from this, restrictions imposed by monetary authorities, for example: no payment of interest to be made on current account, was not applicable for such deposits.

Absence of these restrictions made the deposits attractive not only to the depositors but also to the banks. Such deposits were parked in developing countries debt at attractive returns by the banks and much heed was not paid to credit risk involved in such decisions. This led to the Latin American debt crisis in the late eighties. Discounted convertible bonds much below the face value to the holders of these debt, as per the suggestion given by Mr. Nicholas Brady, US secretary of state, to tide over the crisis, were popularly called as *Brady Bonds*.

Euro Market also had no lender of last resort, which made the market risky. Even though this market mellowed considerably after Latin American debt crisis, it is proving to be an important source of external finance.

In 1957 first step was taken towards the formation of Monetary Union in Europe by six countries - Belgium, Netherlands, Germany, Italy, Luxembourg, and France - by signing treaty of Rome and forming European Economic Community. In 1968 the same was converted to

Customs Union wherein the members adopted single tariff wall for imports from outside the union.

EEC was converted to Common Market in 1993. Many other members like Britain, Denmark, Sweden, Ireland, Finland, Greece, Spain, Portugal, and Austria joined, increasing the membership to 15. In 1991 after drastically amending treaty of Rome, European Economic Community was converted to European Community. In 1999 single currency Monetary Union was formed. While Britain, Sweden and Denmark opted out of the same, Greece was not found eligible.

The structure of European Monetary Union consists of European Parliament, European Council of ministers and European Central bank. European Union faced several acid tests, during German unification. Germany had to increase its money supply to control inflation arising out of increased money supply to facilitate control of inflation. Other members found it difficult to follow up for the fear of increasing recession and unemployment in their economies, leading to attack on their currencies. Countries like Britain, Sweden and Denmark opted out of EU. In spite of that, it will not be wrong to say that the credit goes to the Union that it withstood all the turbulence and Euro emerged as alternative currency to US$.

Introduction of Euro currency is a unique political experiment in which the currency integrates without political integration. Euro has already challenged US$ in trade. Many countries hold now their reserves in Dollar and Euro instead of predominantly being held in US$. Euro can be considered to be much more stable with European Central bank being much freer from member states with clear mandate to maintain inflation level than US Fed. Corporates dealing with Euro will have to invoice in Euro instead of Dollars as they were doing hitherto. Since the introduction of single currency, there is a huge reduction in Hedging cost in Euro zone therefore members competing with Euro zone have to be much more cost competitive. Euro zone has huge surplus and offers very good market for borrowers and issuers of international financial instruments. Seeing the advantage of Euro zone even Britain which stayed outside due to the US influence is increasingly willing to join and preparing itself for the same.

European Central bank has the main objective of controlling inflation and maintaining price stability. Since Euro currency is for a zone which consists of several countries European Central bank is circumscribed to take action involving rise or fall in interest rate in order to stall adverse exchange rate movement. This was evidenced in

1992 itself when UK wanted Germany to lower interest rates, but Germany was not in a position to oblige due to increase in money supply due to higher unification costs. This ultimately led to the famous attack on Pound Sterling leading to withdrawal of Pound Sterling from ERM. This clearly shows the delicate stand ECB had to take keeping in mind all members of the zone.

3.6 INDIAN EXCHANGE RATE SYSTEM

Since Indian Rupee is not traded in International market, there is a concept called *Intervention Currency*. Immediately after independence since India's trading was with Britain and other commonwealth countries in Pound Sterling, Pound Sterling was taken as intervention currency. Value of Rupee was determined against Pound Sterling in inter-bank market and since Rupee was not traded in international market, the value of other currencies was determined against Pound Sterling in international market and the value against Rupee was determined through crossing.

In 70s keeping with India's changing trading composition, Indian Rupees value was determined against other currencies through a basket of currencies reflecting India's changing trading pattern. Pound was still kept as intervention currency.

Indian Exchange Market was tightly controlled by RBI. In 1992 keeping up with the spirit of liberalization, Liberalized Exchange Rate Management System (LERMS) was introduced. In LERMS dual exchange rate mechanism was adopted. 60% exchange rate was market determined while the balance 40% was determined officially to take care of bulk imports by the Government.

In 1993 dual exchange rate system was abolished and the entire exchange rate was made market determined. Dollar replaced Pound Sterling as intervention currency.

CONCLUSION

In this chapter various international systems like Fixed Exchange rate system brought in at Bretten Woods, Floating Exchange Rate system, Free Float, Managed Float, market dominated by speculators, emergence of Euro Dollar and other Euro currency markets and their significance as financing vehicle, Monetary Union and emergence of Euro as a currency are discussed. Indian currency system, the concept of exchange control, intervention currency concept, progressive liberalization, capital account convertibility is also touched upon.

SUGGESTED ASSIGNMENTS

1. What does floating rate system mean?
2. What is meant by J-curve effect?
3. Is floating rate system more inflationary than fixed rate system? Explain.
4. What is managed float?
5. What is an efficient market?
6. What is Arbitrage?
7. Briefly explain the changes in the present international monetary system that you consider likely to occur in future and why?
8. Explain the concept of Euro-Dollar Market?
9. What are Euro Markets?
10. Identify three factors responsible for Euro-Dollar Market?
11. What is meant by Euro Currency?
12. What are the important features of Foreign Exchange Market in India?
13. What are cross rates/synthetic rates?
14. What is two tier foreign exchange market or dual exchange rate system?

Chapter 4

Foreign Exchange Arithmetic

4.1 EXCHANGE RATE ARITHMETIC

There are various types of exchange rates such as: Spot rate, Ready rate, Tom rate, and Forward rate. The date on which currencies are delivered is called as *value date*. In the case of spot transactions, delivery date is two days after the date of transaction (provided the date is a working day in all the centers where transactions are concluded). If that date is a holiday, in any one of the centers, then the subsequent date is the value date.

In the case of Tom rate, the value date is one day after the transaction. All other conditions applicable as mentioned above will be common. In Ready rate transaction value date is same as that of transaction date. Forward rates are rates at which a currency is allowed to be delivered at some future date.

Card rates are rates quoted for a retail customer, while for corporates who deal in bulk special rates are quoted. Card rate is not an exchange rate, it is an approximate rate quoted.

Like in any other commodity, dealers in foreign exchange quote, buy, and sell rates for foreign exchange also. A person dealing in any commodity makes his money by buying at a low rate and selling at a high rate. Buying rate is called as *bid rate* and selling rate is called as *ask rate*. Spread between buying and selling rate is the *dealer's profit* which depends on volume traded and the nature of competitiveness. It is called as *bid ask spread* or simply *spread*.

There are various other rates like Bill rate, TT rate, Mail rate, and Draft rate. Exchange rate depends on the commission which the dealers build into the same. In a Bill rate since the remitter or receiver is asked to verify documents maximum commission is built. In clean transactions since no documents are required to be verified and only amount is required to be remitted, minimum commission is built into the same. Similarly, faster the transfer cheaper will be the exchange rate since interest element to be built into the transaction is minimum and the fluctuation in exchange due to time period is also minimum. Thus, TT rate is cheaper than Draft or Mail rate. TT buying rate is the cheapest quote.

There are two types of quotes internationally–one is called as *American Quote* and other is called as *European Quote*. In American quote for one unit of other currency, number of units of US$ are quoted, while in European quote for one unit of US$, number of units of other currency are quoted.

In Asia direct and indirect quotes are being followed. In direct quote number of units of domestic currency for one units of foreign currency is quoted, while in indirect quote number of unit of foreign currency for predetermined amount of domestic currency is quoted. India followed indirect quote till 1993 before switching to direct quote. To facilitate exports Reserve Bank of India has fixed maximum transit time for direct as well indirect transfer of export documents. Many criticize the RBI Reserve policy. According to critics RBI is building high interest rate reserves which earn very little interest, which is wasteful use of resource.

4.2 EXAMPLES

An exporter has to surrender $ 1,00,000 to a bank. Rate of Dollar against Rupee is 46/46.15, the bank charges a commission of .15%. If the transit time fixed by RBI is 20 days and the rate of interest charged by the bank is 10%,

a) Find out the net proceeds to be credited to exporters account.

Since the exporter sells the dollar to bank bid rate of Rs. 46 per dollar to be taken. Since it involves buying of dollar by bank, commission should be deducted from exchange rate.

Rate to be adopted is (46*.9985) = Rs.45.93

Total amount is $ 1,00,000 * 45.93 = 45,93,000.

Interest charged is 10% for 20 days on the net proceeds. Which is 45,93,000*.10*20/365= Rs.25167

Net proceeds to be credited to the account of exporter = 4593000–25167 = Rs.4567833

b) Find out what is the amount to be paid by the person if he is an importer instead of exporter?

Since in this case the bank is selling the dollar to the importer, it charges the ask rate of 46.15 and the commission is added instead of being deducted. Amount to be paid by the importer.

Rs. 46.15* 1.0015 = Rs.46.22 thus the amount to be paid by the importer to bank is,

$ 1,00,000 * 46.22 = Rs.46,22,000

c) Transaction is concluded spot on March 17, 2003 for US $ 1,00,000 what is the value date?

Value date is 19th March 2003, if it is not a holiday in India or US.

d) What will happen if 19th March is a holiday in US?

Then 20th March, if it is working day in both the centers will be adopted as value date.

e) If an Indian bank sells to a German bank $ 1,00,000 for Belgian Franc what is the value date in this case ?

Value date is 19th March 2003, if it is not a holiday in any one of the transaction centers/settlement centers like India, Germany, US or Belgium or next working day in all the four transaction centers will be the value date.

f) If the above transaction is concluded on 29th March 2003 and 31st March 2003 is a holiday in India, what will be the value date?

April 1st will be value date. Next month rule applies for Forward and not for spot transaction.

g) If Rupee $ rate is 46/46.15 $/ Pound rate is 1.71/1.74 what is Rupee Pound rate.

Rs./Pound rate is = Rs/$ * $/Pound rate

= 46*1.71/ 46.15*1.74

= 78.66/80.30.

h) If French Franc $ is 10.17/ 10.20 and Swiss Franc $ rate is 1.73/1.75 find out French Franc /Swiss Franc Rate?

French Franc / Swiss Franc Rate is = French Franc/$ * $/ Swiss Franc Rate.

$/ Swiss Franc rate is = 1/1.75/1/1.73

= .5714/.5780

French Franc/ Swiss Franc Rate = 10.17*.5714/10.20*.5780

= 5.81/5.90

i) If one Rupee can buy 3.23 Yen and if one rupee can buy .028 dollars, how many yens can one dollar buy?

.028$ = 3.23 Yen

$ = 3.23/.028

= 115.35 Yen.

j) In London a dealer quotes DM/POUND Spot = 3.2550/55, Yen/ Pound spot is = 180/181. What do you expect Yen/DM rate in Frankfurt?

Yen/ DM spot rate is = Yen/ Pound spot Rate * Pound/ DM spot Rate.

DM/Pound Spot rate is = 3.2550/55

Pound/ DM Spot rate is = 1/3.2555/1/3.2550

= .3071/.3072

Yen/DM Spot rate = 180*.3071/181*.3072

= 55.278/55.6032

Suppose that in Frankfurt you get a quote of Yen/DM spot 51.1530/51.2550 is there an arbitrage opportunity?

Buy one DM in Frankfurt by selling 51.2550 yen sell one DM and get 55.278 yen there by making profit of 55.278- 51.2550= 4.023 Yen.

k) February 24 1999, a customer requested a Bank to remit DG 2,50,000 to Holland as payment for Diamonds, However due to strike the Bank can make payment only on March 1, 1999.

InterBank Rates are as follows.

	Feb 24 1999	March 1 1999
Bombay	$/Rs (100Rs) 3.10/3.15	3.07/3.12
London	$/Pound 1.7250/60 DG/Pound 3.9575/90	1.7175/85 3.9380/90

How much does the customer stand to gain or lose due to delay?

Rs/DG = Rs/ $ *$/DG.

Rs/$ 100/3.15/100/3.10 100/3.12/100/3.07

31.75/32.26 32.05/32.57

$/DG=$/PS*PS/DG 1.7250/3.9590/1.7260/3.9575
1.7175/3.9390/1.7185/3.938.

.4357/.4361 .4360/.4364

Rs/DG = 31.75*.4357/32.26*.4361
32.05*.4360/32.57*.4364

13.83/14.07 13.97/14.21

The importer has lost (14.21–14.07)*2,50,000 DG = Rs. 35000 due to delayed remittance.

l) Set out below is a table of cross rates.

	D.M.	Dollar	French Franc	Pound Sterling
Frankfurt	---------	2.2812	4712	4.0218
New York	.4421	--------	.2110	1.8000
Paris	2.0949	4.7393	-------	8.4301
London	4.0207	1.7775	8.4232	-------

Note that the Frankfurt, New York and Paris all quotes are direct, for London all quotes are indirect.

m) If all the above quotes are available at the same time and assuming transaction cost how a nimble trader might take advantage of the situation.

Direct Quote means per Foreign Currency unit how many units of domestic currency and vice versa is true for domestic currency.

To convert Direct Quote to indirect quote.

Frankfurt DM. --------1/2.2812= .4383$
2.1222(FF) .2486(PS)

In Frankfurt pay .4383$ and get one DM sell DM in New York get .4421$. Buy DM in Paris by paying 2.0949 French Franc and sell the same in Frankfurt at 1/.4712 FF 2.1222 .In the same way others can also be done.

n) An Indian Bank has sold 1,00,000 AUD to Indian Importer.

Quote for Rupee/$ in Indian Interbank market = 50/50.5

AUD/ $ Quoted in New York market is = 1.92/ 1.94

How much is the quote Indian Bank should make to Indian importer if it's commission is .15%

Rs/ AUD = Rs/ $ * $/AUD

= 50 * 1/1.94 / 50.5 * 1/1.92 = 25.77/ 26.30

Rate to be quoted to Indian importer

26.30 * 1.0015= 26.34 Rs/ AUD.

CONCLUSION

In this chapter, various concepts of exchange rate like TT rate, Bill rate, Spread, Spot rate, Ready rate, Forward rate, Tom rate, Spread, Direct quote, Indirect quote, American Quote, European Quote, Cross rate or Synthetic rate, Value date are all discussed.

SUGGESTED ASSIGNMENT

1. What is meant by value date?

Chapter 5

Exchange Rate theories and Exchange rate Forecasting

5.1 INTRODUCTION

Swedish Economist Gustav Cassel propounded that the exchange rate is determined on the purchasing power of the currency and the theory is called as *Purchasing Power Parity Theory*. To put it simply, let us consider this, if one US $ can purchase one MacDonald's hamburger, while one hamburger can be purchased for Rs. 50 then one US$= Rs.50.

According to PPP theory all goods are tradable. It assumes presence of a perfect market and the absence of transaction cost, trade barriers like tariff, transportation cost, which are unrealistic.

To generalize, the rate of exchange is determined by the inflation rates of the respective countries. The currency of the country with higher inflation will depreciate and vice versa. For example if one US $ = Rs. 50 and the next year rate in India and US is 10% and 2% respectively as per the *purchasing power parity* theory after one year the rate of exchange between US$ and Indian rupee will be 1$ = 50*(1.10)/(1.02)= Rs. 53.92 otherwise there is scope for arbitraging.

Suppose if the exchange rate from one currency to another is 52, a person in India purchases 1.02$ at Rs. 52 per dollar. With that Rs. 53.04 he purchase items in US and brings them to India. He sells these items at Rs. 55 and makes a riskless profit of Rs 1.96. This process will continue whereby demand for dollar will increase and hence the dollar will appreciate till it reaches Rs.53.92. This concept explains that the difference in exchange rate is nothing but difference in the inflation rate.

Suppose 1$ = Rs.54 and after one year a person in US purchases Rs. 55 for 55/54= 1.0185$, uses it to purchase goods in India, sells the same in US and makes a riskless profit of .0015$. This process will continue thereby demand for rupee will increase hence leading to the appreciation of rupee against dollar till it reaches Rs. 53.92.

There is not much empirical evidence in favour of PPP due to the presence of transaction and transportation costs. The basket of goods used for measuring inflation in different countries is different such as presence of tariff, non-tariff, and trade barriers, taxes, imperfect knowledge and presence of large number of non-tradable (items which cannot be traded internationally like land etc.)

PPP assumptions are valid in a market dominated by fundamental forces like Central bank, Government etc. but in a market dominated by speculators who are on the look out for short term returns, if the inflation in a country rises in short term, hot money flows in the country in anticipation of the interest rate hike. Thus, the currency appreciates instead of depreciating as suggested by PPP.

Therefore, in markets like India where exchange control is in force and exchange rates are still managed by Central bank, the band for depreciation of currencies is set by RBI which is based on inflation rate prevailing in different countries. The exchange rate difference before adjusting inflation difference is called *Nominal Effective Exchange Rate*, while exchange rate difference after adjusting inflation difference is called as *Real Effective Exchange Rate* (NEER, REER respectively).

According to *interest rate parity theory*, the difference in exchange rate is explained by difference in the interest rate. Thus, if one year interest rate on dollar is 6% and one year interest rate on rupee is 12%, present spot rate between rupee and dollar is 1$= Rs.50. A person will borrow in dollar and invest in rupee. After one year he has to pay back 1.06$ and he will get Rs.56. Interest rate parity theory suggests that the exchange rate between dollar and rupee should be 1.06$= Rs.56 or 1$ = 56/1.06 = 52.83, otherwise there is scope for arbitrage. Interest rate parity theory assumes no exchange control, absence of transaction cost and taxes, perfect market.

Interest rate before adjusting for inflation is called as *Nominal Interest Rate* and interest rate after adjusting for inflation is called as *Real Interest Rate*. Under international Fischer effect, real interest rate across the world determines the difference in exchange rate, otherwise there will be scope for arbitrage. Ultimately, Fischer effect states that real interest rate across the world should converge otherwise there will be scope for arbitrage. Exchange rates are also determined by demand and supply and psychological factors. All these factors act on simultaneous basis to determine exchange rates.

5.2 EXCHANGE RATE DETERMINATION PROBLEMS

To explain the exchange rate determination, let us consider some problems:

1. If the current Rs/ $ rate is Rs. 50, one year inflation rate is 10% for rupee and 2% for dollar. If one year later, the rate of exchange between dollar and rupee in forward rate is Rs.55, is there scope for arbitrage, if PPP is applicable?

   As per PPP one year later rate will be = (50*1.10)/1.02= 53.92, since the present forward rate is not in alignment, he can sell the dollar forward.

2. Spot Exchange rate between Rs/$ 50, if annual inflation rate is 10% in India and 3% in US, what will be the rate of return to Indian investor if the return on US security is 10% if PPP is applicable?

   Indian Investor can convert Rs. 50 to one dollar and invest the same in US security. After one year he will get 1.10 $. One year later the applicable exchange rate under PPP theory will be,

   $ = 50*1.10/1.03= 53.40 Rs .

   1.10$ will be equivalent to 1.10* 53.40 = 58.74 thus the rate of return to Indian investor is (58.74-50/50)*100 that is 17.48%.

3. In the above case if the percentage of return in India is 10% what is the rate of return to American Investor?

   American investor can convert one dollar to Rs.50 and invest the same in Indian market. After one year he will get Rs. 50* 1.10= Rs. 55, if this is converted to dollars it will be 1.03$, so the rate will be 3% for American investor.

4. Following is the data relating to spot rate, forward rate and money market rates. Compute the missing value if the covered interest parity holds good.

Spot Rate Rs/$	3m Forward Rate Rs/$	Interest Rate US $	Interest Rate Rs
33.50	33.80	–2.36	6%
33.70	33.40	6%	2.4%
33.50	33.67	4%	6%
33.16	33.80	4%	6%

If interest Rate parity holds good

33.50(1.015)/(1+I)= 33.80

1+I = 33.50(1.015)/33.80

I= .9941–1= 59*4= 2.36

33.70(1+I)/(1.015)= 33.40

1+I = 33.40*1.015/33.70= 1.0060

I = .0060

33.50*1.015/1.01= 33.67

33.80*(1.04)/1.06= 33.16

5. The following rates are given

$/pound spot 1.5625/35

Euro $ deposit 81/4/81/2

Euro Pound Deposit 12/13.

What are the limits of forward quote where there will be no covered interest arbitrage opportunities?

Bid rate Borrow Pound at 13%, convert to Dollar at 1.5625 invest at 81/4% after one year rate

1.13 pounds = 1.6914$

Pound = 1.6914/1.13= 1.4968 $ bid rate after one year,

Borrow 1.5635$ at 81/2% dollar, convert to Pound invest at 12% interest, after one year

1.5635*(1.085)= 1.12

1.6965 $ = 1.12 pound

1 Pound = 1.5147

Thus the bid ask rate after one year to provide no arbitrage opportunity is $/ pound 1.4968/1.5147

6. You have been given the following information.

RUS 15%, RUK 16% S($/Pound) 2 F1/4($/POUND) 1.995

Where RUS annual interest rate on 3 months US Commercial Paper.

RUK is annual interest rate on UK Commercial paper.

S($/Pound) = number of US$ /Pound spot.

F1/4($/Pound) = number of US$ per pound 3 months forward.

a. Where would you invest? (Invest in UK),

b. Where would you borrow? (Borrow in US).

c. How would you arbitrage?

Borrow 2$ at 3.75% for three months, invest in one pound at 4% in UK

Interest rate parity after three months

2*(1.0375) = 1*1.04

2.075 = 1.04PS

1PS= 2.075/1.04

= 1.9951

Since the exchange rate confirms interest rate parity principle no covered interest arbitrage is possible.

7. An American Mutual is planning to invest 10 million dollars either in India or in Hong Kong. For one year which is holding period, expected rate of return in India is 18%, rate of return in Hong Kong is 15%.

Spot Rate

Rs/ Us$ = 49.50/50

HK$/ US$ = 4/ 4.1

Rate of inflation

India	6%
HK	4%
US	2%

Tax in India 20%, tax in Hong Kong 10%

PPP theory will apply.

If PPP is applicable exchange rate after one year will be

Rs/ US$ = 49.5* 1.06/1.02 : 50*1.06/1.02

= 51.44/ 51.96

HK$/ US$ = 4*1.04/1.02 : 4.1*1.04/1.02

= 4.08/ 4.18

Amount invested in Indian Rupee = $ 1,00,000,00* 49.5= 49,50,000,00

After one year amount of return = 49,50,000,00* .18= 89100000

After tax return = 89100000* .80 = 71280000

Total amount to be repatriated = 566280000/(51.96)$ = 10898384 $

Rate of return = 8.98%

Amount to be invested in HK$ = 10000000* 4= 4,00,00000

RETURN = 4,00,00000* .15= 60,00,000 HK$

Tax = 60,00,000* .1= 6,00,000 HK$

Amount to be repatriated after one year = 4,54,00,000/ 4.18 US $= 108612244

Rate of return = 8.61%

Thus it is better to invest in India than in Hong Kong.

8. A Limited company has a requirement for Rs. 5 crores. Rate of interest for borrowing in Indian Rupee is 16% p.a. While if the same is borrowed in dollar Spot rate is Rs/$ = 50/50.5 and sixth month forward is 53/54. Borrowing in dollars attracts interest rate of 8% p.a. In which currency he should borrow. Find the dollar interest rate at which he will be indifferent to borrowings in rupee and dollar?

If he borrows in Rupees, interest after six months is

5,00,000,00 * .16/2 = 40,00,000.

If he borrows in Dollar initial borrowing is 1 million $

Principle plus interest to be repaid in $ is

10,00,000 * (1.04) = 10,40,000.

Remittance of $ in terms of rupee is 10,40,000* 54 = 56160000

Thus excess payment is 21,60,000 under $ borrowing.

Thus rupee borrowing is preferred.

Let the six months $ interest rate be 'I'

10,00,000*(1.i)* 54 = 54000000

Thus at nil interest only the $ loan will be indifferent to Rupee loan.

9. If Rs/ Euro Spot is Rs/ Euro = 52/53

6 month forward is = 54/55

Inflation rate in India 6%

Inflation rate in Eurozone is 2%

Find the real and nominal appreciation / depreciation of Rupee and Euro.

Nominal rate of appreciation of Euro = 2/52* 2* 100/ 2/53* 2*100

= 7.79%/ 7.55%

Real rate of Rs. against euro = 54* 1.02/1.06= 51.96/ 55* 1.02/1.06= 52.92

Real depreciation of Euro = (52-51.96/52)*2*100) = .15%

= (53- 52.92/53)*2 *100)= .30%

= .15%/.30%

Nominal depreciation of Rupee

Euro/rupee spot = 1/53/ 1/52

= .0189/ .0192

Euro rupee forward

= 1/55/ 1/54

= .0182/ .0185

Nominal depreciation of rupee = (.0189-.0182/.0189) * 2*100/ (.0192- .0185/ .0192) * 2* 100

57

= 7.41%/ 7.29%

Real rate of Euro/ Rupee = 1/52.92/ 1.51.96

= .0189/ .0192

Practically, there is very little appreciation of real rate of Rupee against Euro.

10. A U.K subsidiary of a US Parent can borrow from UK at a cost of 8%, while from the parent it can borrow at 6%, from Germany it can borrow at 7% interest rate parity theory holds good, for all borrowings 20% with holding. tax is applicable. Where from the company should borrow?

Cost of borrowing from UK = 8%

Borrowing From US = 6%

Net of with holding tax = 6/.8= 7.5

Exchange premium= 1.06/1.08= .98

Thus cost of borrowing from US = 7.5+ .98 = 8.48%

Borrowing from Germany = 7%

Net of with holding tax = 8.75%

Exchange rate premium = 1.07/1.08=.99%

Cost of borrowing from Germany = 8.75+ .99 = 9.74%

Thus it is cheaper to borrow from UK itself.

11. If the rupee $ spot rate and forward rate are given

Rs/$ = 50/51

Rs/$ 6 months forward rate = 53/54

Six months interest rate in India = 18%/18.5%

6 month interest rate in US $ = 6/ 6.5%

is there an opportunity for arbitrage?

Borrow 1$ at 6.5% convert to rupee at Rs. 50 spot invest in 18%.

After 6 months investment will yield 50* 1.09 = 54.5

1$ to be repaid at 1.065/2= 1.0325 $

1.0325$ after 6 months is = 1.0325 *54 = 55.76

Thus, there is no scope for arbitrage through this route.

Borrow 51 Rs at 18.5% covert it to $ and invest at 6%.

After 6 months amount to be repaid in rupee = (51* (1.0925) = 55:72

1$ will yield after 6 months 1.03$ in terms of rupee is = 1.03* 53

= 54.59 Rs

There is no scope for arbitrage.

12. If Rs/$ = 50

Inflation 7% India and 3% US

Real appreciation is 5% for US $

What is exchange rate after six months?

Nominal appreciation of US $ = 50* 1.07/1.03= 51.94

Actual exchange rate = 51.94*1.05= Rs.54.54

13. Spot Rs/$ 50/50.5

US interest rate: 5/5.5

Interest rate in Rupees: 10. /10.5

Quote six months forward rate with no scope for covered interest arbitrage.

Borrow 1$ at 5.5% interest convert to Rupee at Rs. 50 invest at 10%

1*(1. (.055/2)= 50* 1.1/2

1.0275$ = 52.5

1$ = Rs. 51.09

Borrow Rs. 50.5 at 10.5% convert to dollar and invest at 5%

50.5* (1.0525) = 1.025$

1.025$= 53.15

$ = Rs. 51.85

So the 6 months forward rate to avoid any covered interest arbitrage is = Rs.51.09/ 51.85

14. An Indian company will avail a 1.5 million Euro Loan. It will repay the loan in 3 equal annual installments. Rs/Euro spot rate is 52. If the inflation in Euro zone is 3% and inflation in India is 7% real appreciation in exchange rate of euro is 5%. What is the rupee liability of loan?

1st year exchange rate nominal = 52* (1.07)/1.03= Rs.54.02

Actual exchange rate = 54.02 * 1.05= Rs.56.72

1st year repayment = 500000* 56.72= Rs.28360000

2nd year's exchange rate nominal

56.72* 1.07/1.03= Rs. 58.92

Actual exchange rate = 58.92* 1.05= 61.87

Repayment in second year = 500000* 61.87= Rs.30935000

3rd year's exchange rate nominal.

61.87* 1.07/1.03= Rs.64.27

Actual exchange rate = 64.27* 1.05

= Rs.67.48

Actual rupee liability = 500000* 67.48= Rs. 33740000

15. If the following rates are given

6 months forward = Rs. 52

Interest rate	Rupee	$
6 months	12%	6%
9 months	14%	7%
12 months	15%	8%

What is the third month forward rate from 9th month?

If S is the spot rate

S*(1.12/2) / (1.06/2) = 52

S = 52*1.03/ 1.06

= Rs.50.53

9th month Forward

50.53 * (1.14*3/4) / (1.07*3/4) = 50.53* (1.105)/ (1.0525) = Rs. 53.05

3 month interest rate

(1.14* ¾) (1+ i/4) = 15

(1.105) (1+ i/4) = .15

1+ i/4 = 1.15/ (1.105)

= 1.0472

i/4 = 1.0472-1

= .0472

I = .0472* 4

= .1888

= 18.88% for rupee

(1+ .07* ¾) * (1+ i/4) = 1.08

(1+ .0525) * (1+ i/4) = 1.08

1+ i/4 = 1.08/ 1.0525

= 1.0261

i/4 = 1.0261-1

= .0261

I = .0261* 4

= 10.44% for dollar

12th month forward = 53.05* (1.1888/4)/ (1.1044/4)

= 53.05 * (1.0472)/ (1.0261)

= 54.14

16. Spot rate Rs.50/$

6 month forward Rs. 55/$

If the rupee interest rate 16%

What is $ interest rate

50* (1.16/2)/ (1+i/4) = 55

50* 1.08* (1+ i/4) = 55

54 * (1+ i/4) = 55

1+ i/4 = 55/54

1+ i/4 = 1.0185

i/4 = 1.0185-1

= .0185

I = .074

= 7.4%

5.3 EXCHANGE RATE FORECASTING

Forward rate can be used to predict future exchange rate. Forward rate cannot be perfect predictor of future spot rate since forward rate contains all the current factors and expected changes in exchange rate while unexpected rate cannot be factored in. Exchange rate can be predicted through relative inflation rates as per *Purchasing Power Parity Theory* or through elative interest rate as per *Interest Rate Parity Theory*.

Exchange rate can be predicted by using forces of demand and supply as per Balance of Payment statistics. If the Balance of Payment is negative then demand for foreign currency will increase leading to depreciation of domestic currency vice versa the domestic currency will appreciate. If the GNP of a country increases then the demand will go up, import will increase thereby Balance of Payment will become deteriorated leading to depreciation of currency and vice versa.

In monetary approach, the results are exactly as opposed to Balance of Payment approach. For example: if the real economy of country expands and money supply does not expand then there will be more demand for money than supply leading to its appreciation which is diametrically opposed to Balance of Payment approach. The corrective mechanism is in the form of increase in the interest rate thereby bond prices will drop, due to which it will be costly to hold money and money will be spent for purchasing goods and hence inflation will increase. Since PPP is assumed to be true under this theory value of currency will decrease.

In *Dornbusch Sticky Price Theory*, the extent of appreciation of currency and depreciation of currency due to the above factor is much more warranted than due to the stickiness of price of non-tradable, which subsequently gets rectified due to the non-tradable price, therefore catching up with inflation.

In the *Asset Approach*, since the foreign exchange market is efficient, all the historic news and expected news is reflected in the price, only unexpected news which follows random walk influences the price which cannot be predicted. But Governments of the countries and Central banks who are players in the market do not act with profit motive, so indicators like fiscal deficit, money supply and inflation can be watched for forecasting exchange rate.

Under *Portfolio Balance Approach*, it is assumed that exchange rate is determined by two factors, demand for money and demand for bonds. If the interest rate raises demand for bond rises. To counter this the wealth of bond holder is decreased by appreciating domestic currency, since the appreciation of domestic currency decreases the wealth of bond holder for bond he holds in foreign currency, vice versa explains depreciation of the currency.

Exchange rate can also be predicted by using technical analysis wherein movement in exchange rate itself can be used to predict future exchange rates as per certain well observed patterns. Technical analysts are called as astrologers of the foreign exchange markets. Fundamentalists and Economist forcefully disagree with them, since the *Efficient Market Theory* says that foreign exchange being an efficient market, all historic costs and future expectations are reflected in the price. Since the price moves due to unexpected news which occurs on random walk basis, historic data is of very little help in predicting the future movements of exchange rates. But Chartists have, many a times, in the past, used historic data to predict future movements in price.

CONCLUSION

In these problems, we studied about Purchasing Power Parity Theory which says that the difference in exchange rate is explained by difference in inflation; Interest Rate Parity Theory which says that difference in exchange rate is due to difference in interest rate; International Fischer theory explains that difference in exchange rate is due to difference in real interest rate which will ultimately converge. Forecasting Exchange rates use demand and supply approach. Monetary approach, portfolio balancing approach, Dornbusch Sticky Price Theory as well as technical analysis are explained.

SUGGESTED ASSIGNMENTS

1. What is Purchasing Power Parity Theory?
2. What is International Fischer Effect? What is the rationale for it's existence?
3. Why do Foreign Exchange Rates vary?
4. What is covered interest arbitrage?
5. What is meant by NEER and REER?
6. Explain the rationale behind Purchasing Power Parity Theory?

Chapter 6

Exchange Risk Management

6.1 INTRODUCTION

A firm may have its assets and liabilities denominated in currencies other than that of its own. Due to the fluctuation in the exchange rate between time from which such risk is contracted and settled, there will be an effect on the profits of the firm (whether favourable or adverse), this is called as *Exchange Exposure*.

The recent phenomenon of contagion in South East Asian and Russian crisis forced international regulator to take into account the systemic risk involved in addressing the same. Thus came into existence, the concept of capital adequacy and risk weightage for banks as determined by Basel Committee. The risk models are getting sophisticated and the risk weightage is allotted based on credit rating rather than allocating uniform weightage to each sector. The bias for not attaching weightage to short term lending is being done away with. Since the South East Asian crisis arose out of crony capitalism, increasing steps are being taken to impose Corporate Governance practice throughout the world. Over The Counter or OTC derivatives which are kept as off balance sheet without any requirement for reporting outstanding transaction, were the main reason for LTCM crisis. Therefore, increasingly accounting standards are incorporated to bring it on balance sheet. Transparency is introduced in financial reporting in order to facilitate world investment. Since most of the foreign investment flowed to emerging markets through banks and mismanagement of credit leading to South East Asian crisis, banks are now subject to capital adequacy requirements and stringent measures introduced to enable banks to report their earnings on prudent basis. Apart from this, risk management concepts like Asset Liability Management are introduced in emerging market's banking system.

There are three types of exposures and these are discussed as follows:

6.1.1 Transaction Exposure

Transaction exposure arises due to fluctuation in exchange rate between the time at which the contract is concluded in foreign currency and the time at which settlement is made. Transaction exposure is short term in nature, usually for a period of less than one year.

6.1.2 Translation Exposure

Translation exposure arises due to a company having foreign branches or subsidiaries, which are required to be consolidated with the accounts of the parent branch at the end of the year. These accounting statements are denominated in foreign currency and they have to be converted to domestic currency at the time of consolidation leading to exchange rate exposure, and the exposure is called Translation exposure or Accounting exposure since this exposure is recognized much before the settlement is made. Translation exposure does not involve immediate cash outflow.

6.1.3 Economic Exposure

When a country's economy is increasingly integrated internationally, it is exposed to vagaries of international market even though it may not have any transactions in foreign currency neither in the form of imports, nor in the form of exports. Thus, a firm may not have any transaction in foreign exchange at all but if its competitor firm imports its major raw material and components, say for example in Japanese Yen, the firm is exposed to economic exposure. If Yen depreciates against rupee, then imports from Japan will become cheaper. This benefit can be passed on the customers thereby directly affecting the market share of the other firm.

6.2 EXAMPLES

1. If a person exports 100 pieces of Jewellery to USA and price per piece is 200$, while he imports material from Japan and price per piece is 6000 Yen. If labour rate is Rs. 1000 per piece and variable overhead per piece is Rs. 500 if the spot rate is Rs. 50 per Dollar and 120 yen/dollar and one month later when the exports take place one Dollar = Rs.53 and one Dollar is 110 Yen, compute transaction exposure.

Present sales = (100*200)* 50= 10,00,000

Present cost = (100*6000/120)*50= 2,50,000

Labour = (100*1000) = 1,00,000

Overhead = (100*500) = 50,000

Profit = Rs. 6,00,000.

Sales after a month = (100*200)*53= 10,60,000

One month later cost = (100*6000/110)*53= 289091

Labour = (100*1000) = 1,00,000

Overhead = (100*500) = 50000

Profit = Rs. 620909

Increase in profit due to transaction exposure = 620909–600000
= 20,909.

In the above problem what will be economic exposure, if the company maintains its export price in rupee and price elasticity of demand is 2.

Price per piece before depreciation= 200*50= Rs.10,000

If the exchange rate is Rs. 53 price in dollar is = (10,000/53) = 188.68

Dip in price = 11.32

% of dip in price = 5.66%

Price Elasticity of demand

Increase in demand due to increase in price = 5.66*2= 11.32%.

After dip in price revised demand = (100*1.11)= 111

Revised sales = 111*10,000= 11,10,000

Cost of Materials = (111*6000/110)*53= 320891

(Labour = (111*1000)= 1,11,000

Overhead = (111*500)= 55500

Revised Profit = 6,22,609.

Increase in profit due to Economic exposure = 622609–600000= 22,609.

2. An Exporter is exporting 100 articles for 50$ each and importing the 100 units of material at 10 Euros. He incurs other variable expenses of Rs. 20,000. At the time of entering into the contract Rs/$ = 47 at the time of export it is 46 while Rs/Euro at the time of order is Rs. 50 while at the time of export is Rs. 53. If the price elasticity of the goods is 1.5, what are the Transaction and the Economic exposure?

Transaction exposure:

100* 50 * 1 = –5000 for exports in $

For imports in Euro is 100* 10* 3= –3000 Rs

Thus total transaction exposure is – 8000.

Economic exposure:

If instead of dollar invoicing the entity has done invoicing in Rupees

Each item will cost = 50* 47/46 = 51$. A two per cent increase in price would have led to 3% decline in Demand that is 97.

Original Profits	= 100* 50* 47 – 20,000–10* 100* 50
	= Rs. 1,65,000.
Revised Profit	= 97* 51* 46 – 20000* 97/100–10* 97* 53
	= 227562–19400–51410 = 156752.

Loss due to Economic Exposure = 156752–165000= 8248Rs.

6.3 FOREIGN EXCHANGE RISK

Many a times foreign exchange risk is used synonymously with foreign exchange exposure. This is not correct. Foreign Exchange exposure arises due to firms, assets and liabilities denominated in currencies which are different from domestic currency. Due to the fluctuation between the date on which the contract is concluded and the settlement is made, the effect is visible on the firm's profit and loss and thus the exposure is called as foreign exchange exposure. But the foreign exchange risk can be defined like any other risk as the difference between the actual exchange rate and the anticipated exchange rate.

Foreign Exchange market is increasingly becoming an efficient market due to which past behaviour cannot be used to anticipate the future. Once upon a time the idea was, risk elimination. But in an efficient market, one cannot get above-average returns without taking risk. Thus, today the emphasis is more on risk management that is keeping risk within the acceptable limits of the organization rather than risk elimination.

There are other risks like unsystematic risks, which can be reduced or eliminated through diversification in securities which are not perfectly positively correlated. Systematic risk is that kind of risk which cannot be eliminated by portfolio investment.

Various types of risks are defined as follows:

6.3.1 Systematic Risk

Systematic risk is the risk occurring at one point, which spreads to the other points because of the global integration phenomena, and is called as *contagion*. Various measures like capital adequacy, disclosure, effective financial supervision and corporate governance are used against Systematic risk.

6.3.2 Market Risk

Market risk in derivative trade is due to the movement in the price of underlying, which affects the price of derivatives adversely.

6.3.3 Liquidity Risk

Liquidity risk occurs more in the case of Over The Counter (OTC) derivatives, which due to the non-standard structure makes it to have no secondary market. Hence, liquidity risk is there to adversely affect the parties, ability to get over undesirable position. This is done by commoditizing OTC derivatives and warehousing and selling them as in the case of Swap* being standardized by ISDA**.

---

*Please refer topic 7.13 for full details of Swap.

** Go to Glossary for the full form.

6.3.4 Interest Rate Risk

Interest rate risk is due to the rise or fall in the fixed interest rate risk on the fixed income security as well as on the stock of money held.

6.3.5 Legal Risk

Legal risk is due to many instruments like Forward Rate agreement, which in simple terms is nothing but betting on interest rate. It has the danger of courts in various countries declaring them illegal as *wager*. Thus, the OTC market tries to overcome through standardizing various instruments like swap across the globe, through the procedures like netting, coordinating and imposing uniform regulations on derivatives throughout the world.

6.3.6 Operation Risk

Operation risk exists due to inadequate control procedures like front and back office function not being separated or no effective internal audit function, no proper MIS or monitoring of treasury operations, no well laid out risk management policy by the top management and the top management salaries being excessively linked to treasury operations.

6.3.7 Counter Party Risk

Counter Party risk arises due to heavy concentration of derivative positions with few counter parties, absence of information about the credit worthiness of the counter party, and /or derivatives being kept as off balance sheet items.

6.3.8 Combined Risk

All these risks not only influence individually but also influence in combination. Various models are being given for risk measurement and these models of techniques for measuring risk are called as *Risk metrics*. They are subjected to tests like stress testing and simulation.

6.4 CENTRALIZED AND DECENTRALIZED SYSTEM FOR MANAGING RISK

The process of international integration along with t availability of communication technology has facilitated the process of Risk Management. The importance of risk management is increasingly being recognized with global integration wherein hitherto available protective walls are removed. This evidenced in our own country where many banks, of late, adopted Asset Liability Management (ALM) technique. There are various methods of managing risks, they are given below:

6.4.1 Netting

If the firm is involved in both imports and exports and if the imports and exports are taking place in the same currency then it acts as an automatic/natural hedge, subject to timing difference. Netting is extensively used by MNCs with branches across the world, wherein one branch may have receivables in a particular currency, and the other branch may have payables in the same currency, the head office manages the same on net basis on pooling method.

6.4.2 Leading

If the domestic currency is expected to depreciate against foreign currency then payments are preponed but realization of the exports is postponed, vice versa is true for exports.

6.4.3 Lagging

If domestic currency is expected to appreciate against foreign currency, payments are postponed while receipts are preponed.

6.4.4 Sourcing

If sourcing of the material is shifted to a third currency, the adverse effect of exchange rate appreciation on export competitiveness is mitigated by sourcing goods from the importing country itself or from countries whose currencies are not appreciating.

6.4.5 Relocation

By relocating manufacturing facility in a country whose currency does not appreciate, export competitiveness can be enhanced. Under this method exchange rate management becomes strategic and comes within the purview of top management instead of treasury function.

6.4.6 Having Multicurrency Assets/ Liabilities

This is based on the simple adage: "don't put all eggs in one basket". If assets and liabilities are denominated in different currencies the adverse fluctuation in one currency will be cancelled by favourable fluctuation in the other currency.

6.4.7 Invoicing in Third Currency

Indian exchange rates against all currencies are determined through the medium of US Dollar which is the intervention currency. Thus, there are two fluctuations involved in any other currency against rupee is a multiple of variance of rupee against dollar and dollar against other currency as against single variance of rupee against dollar. Thus, for an Indian dealing in any foreign exchange, it is advantageous to invoice in dollar to minimize exchange rate fluctuation. The same principle of third currency invoicing for managing exchange risk is applied here.

6.4.8 Money Market Hedge

In Money Market hedge, if payables are there then money can be borrowed at local market and can be converted at the local rate and invested abroad for the period of payable. From the proceeds of investment payables can be paid. Similarly, if he is an exporter he can borrow at the foreign market convert it at the spot rate and invest in domestic market. From the proceeds of export he can repay foreign loan. Money market hedges are useful for managing Transaction exposure.

6.5 EXAMPLES

1. If a person has to make payment of US$ 1,00,00C .ter 3 months. Interest Rate in India for 3 months is 10% P.A. and in US is 6% P.A. Spot Rate is 1$= Rs. 46. If third month forward rate is Rs.47, is it worthwhile to go for money market hedge or Forward market hedge?

   If one wants to do money market hedge borrow in Indian Market which will be equivalent to 1,00,000$ after 3 months, that is (1,00,000/1.015)= 98522 US$. Equivalent Indian rupee Rs. 4532012. After three months 1,00,000$ will be received and will be used for settlement of payable. Amount to be paid in Indian Rupee (4532012* 1.025) = Rs. 4645312 while for Forward cover amount of liability is 4700000 Rs. Thus money market hedge is preferable.

   In the above problem if instead of importer, an exporter is there what should be the hedge, he will adopt if the third month interest rate in US $ is 6/6.5% spot Rs/$ exchange rate is 45.50/46 and Rupee interest rate for 3 months is 9.5%/10%, 3 month forward rate is 46.75/47 what will be your decision?

   He borrows that amount which will become 1,00,000 $ after 3 months. That is at a rate of 6.5% P.A. for three months being the ask rate. (100000/1.01625) = 98401$, convert in rupee at spot on bid rate that is 45.50 Rs/$ that is (98401*45.50= Rs. 4477245). After three months out of export proceeds Dollar loan can be paid.

   After 3 months amount of rupee available will be at 9.5% P.A.

   (4477245*(1.02375) = Rs. 4583580 While he will receive Rs.46,75,000 in forward market. Thus, the amount received under forward market is higher than money market thus forward market is preferable to money market.

2. A imports 1,00,000 $ and the supplier offers him a 6 months credit at a rate of interest of 6%, interest rate on overdraft in India is 12%, if the spot rupee dollar rate is Rs.46 and sixth month Forward rate is Rs. 49, is it worthwhile to accept the proposal.

   If the proposal is not accepted amount payable now is Rs. 46,00,000 while interest at 12% for 6 months will be Rs.48,76,000 while if the proposal is accepted amount payable is (1,00,000*1.03= 1,03.000* 49= 50,47,000). So not accepting the proposal is the decision.

CONCLUSION

In this chapter various types of exposures like Transaction exposure, Translation exposure, Economic exposure and risks like legal risk, liquidity risk, interest rate risk, and counter party risk are discussed. Various ways of managing risks like netting, leading, lagging, sourcing, setting up investment outside the country are also discussed.

SUGGESTED ASSIGNMENTS

1. What is meant by Exchange Exposure? How it is different from Exchange Risk?
2. What is meant by Accounting Exposure?
3. What is Money Market Hedge? Illustrate how it can be employed.

Chapter 7

Derivatives

7.1 INTRODUCTION

Derivatives are risk transferring instruments. They are called as derivatives since they derive their value from the value of underlying, which may be either interest rate, foreign exchange, index, commodity or shares or any securities.

Derivatives can be classified as Over the Counter (OTC) derivatives and Exchange Traded Derivatives.

7.1.1 Over the Counter Derivatives

Over the counter derivatives are entered between two individuals or entities, through telephone, telex, fax or personally. They are non-standard and customized, due to which they are illiquid and are subject to counter party risk. They do not facilitate price discovery.

7.1.2 Exchange Traded Derivatives

Exchange Traded Derivatives are standardized in terms of quantity, delivery etc. They are highly liquid, since the clearing house of the exchange acts as guarantor, they are not subject to counter party risk, they facilitate price discovery.

Forwards and Swaps are examples of Over The Counter Derivatives, while Future is an Exchange Traded Derivative. Options are both Over the Counter and Exchange Traded Derivatives.

Even though derivatives are basically risk transfer instruments used for hedging, they are used extensively for speculation, thereby increasing risk instead of reducing the same.

Newspaper reports about the collapse of Barings Bank due to the future trading and position taking in Simex by Mr. Nick Leeson the rogue trader, LTCM crisis, huge loss suffered by Procter & Gamble, Sumitomo Corporation has made public to identify derivatives themselves with risk. But a close reading of situation will make it clear that it was not derivative per se which was responsible for the collapse but elementary factors like absence of internal control such as: Governing body of the organization (the Board) did not fix any limits on position-taking such as: intra day position, overnight position, and the Top Management salary was excessively linked to speculative treasury profits. Also, because of the factors like: the back office functions reporting to operations and absence of the formal internal audit had led to the situation than derivatives themselves.

7.3 BARINGS BANK DEBACLE

In the case of Barings Bank, rogue trader Nick Leeson felt that Yen is overvalued due to short selling of "Yen future". He took a short position in Yen in SIMEX with an idea to cover the same in Japanese stock exchange Nikkie. But instead of Yen falling, it appreciated leading to huge losses. Barings Bank had many weaknesses for example:

The Board of the Company never set a risk policy in the form of laying down intraday and overnight positions. Since the top management salary was hugely variable and linked to the treasury operations profit, they did not want to lay down any risk policy and allowed huge risk to be taken. The back office was asked to report to Nick Leeson. He asked them to put the huge loss in error account which they readily obliged.

Since the Board was totally siding with Nick Leeson, when he asked heavy margin money for trading in future in spite of reporting profits in derivative trading, neither the internal audit department was allowed to scrutinize the treasury function, nor the head office personnel were allowed to question Nick Leeson. Thus, it can be seen that the failure of Barings Bank was not due to derivatives as highlighted in the press but due to absence of elementary internal control.

7.4 DAIWA BANK

In the case of Daiwa Bank Mr. Iguchi was in charge of front and back office. In order to cover up a small loss of 2,00,000$ due to trading in security, he sold some securities. Whenever the investment Banker Baner's Trust sent statement for these sales, Mr.Iguchi used to forge a statement. For eleven long years this continued and ultimately when Mr. Iguchi was replaced, a loss of 1.1 billion $ was found out. Internal Audit never got an independent confirmation from investment banker for eleven long years. Neither elementary control like front and back office separation, and periodic rotation of duty were not implemented nor were the key personnel asked to take leave. Absence of these elementary controls rather than derivatives lead to such a huge loss.

7.5 SUMITOMO DEBACLE

Hamanaka was a copper trader who was given free hand by Sumitomo to trade in copper position. He built long positions in the London Metal Exchange (LME) and held copper price firm at his will till early 90's. But when the US hedge firm started entering this market with huge short sale with the plan to cover the position through future markets Hamanaka was not able to take counter party position any more leading to huge collapse of copper price and consequent loss to Sumitomo. In fact LME copper prices themselves took several years to recover. Again it can be seen that the debacle was not due to derivatives, but due to the company abdicating its responsibility in favour of a star trader.

7.6 LTCM DEBACLE

Long Term Capital Market debacle took place due to the high leveraging of the LTCM fund as well as LTCM taking opposite position like being long on Russian Bond Market expecting Russian rates to fall and took short position in German Bond Market expecting the same to rise. But due to the Russian debt crisis the opposite happened leading to rise in Russian interest rate and fall in German interest rate due to money from Russian Bond market flowing into German market. Thus, LTCM took a double whammy. Due to the huge off balance sheet exposure many banks and financial institutions had with LTCM, the international financial system went on the verge of collapse and Federal Reserve had to intervene. Here again it was due to absence of risk assessment mechanism in bank which led to taking huge counter party exposure with LTCM and the absence of international system for measuring and managing risk led to the disaster rather than derivative trading.

Thus, it can be seen from the above examples that the absence of elementary systems rather than derivatives was the reason for turmoil in the financial system.

OTC derivative market greatly facilitated in managing traders' risk. But unlike in a traditional loan where there is a counter party risk only in a derivative like *swap*, the underlying value of the *swap* changes almost every day and marking the same to market is quite complicated. The volume of trading in OTC market is significant and counter party risk as well as systemic risk is enhanced due to the presence of a few well known players who do majority of the transactions like LTCM. Thus, if one institution is in trouble the contagion spreads quickly to other institutions as it happened in the latest LTCM debacle which added to the systemic risks. Unlike in Exchange Traded Derivative Market, there is no formal clearing or settlement system. Also, the absence of regulatory authority adds to the risk.

OTC derivatives are opaque and are not subject to disclosures. For example a *swap* is neither characterized as security nor as a commodity in United States due to which it is neither regulated by SEC nor by Commodity Trading Board. A *Swap* has two way counter party risk.

The Basel Committee accord capital adequacy acts as a major impediment for Fund based lending. To overcome this bank employs various derivatives to increase their fee-based income. In order to do this, developed *swap* and various complicated derivatives are bought into shape by Physicists and Mathematicians popularly called as Rocket Scientists. These OTC products are quite complicated as evidenced by Procter and Gamble debacle.

The concentration of OTC products with few financial intermediaries is essentially due to high infrastructure requirement by way of investment in technology to deal in these products. This essentially makes the OTC trading concentrate in few institutions making the international financial system susceptible to contagion.

Because of the decentralized risk management, the system for assessing credit risk is quite weak in OTC products. The low margin requirements brought in by competitive pressures collaterals were found to be inadequate to get over the problem during the period of high international turbulence like Russian debt crisis. Model building based on techniques like Value At Risk (VAR) failed during period of increasing international turbulence. High innovation in these markets leads to legal risk where the courts in some countries declare these transactions as *wager* and illegal. These risks along with the liquidity risk are in the process of being overcome by increasingly standardizing OTC like *swap* and making it look like a commodity as in the case of exchange traded derivatives with no guaranteeing mechanism. By doing this netting can be adopted as a mechanism to overcome counter party risks to a certain extent.

Even though the market discipline is considered as one of the methods of regulating OTC market, the fallacy of entirely relying on market discipline was exposed during LTCM crisis where leading financial institutions which built huge counter party exposure with LTCM failed to have any arrangement to share information among them. Even in the post debacle scenario they were never able to agree to a common bailout strategy ultimately forcing Federal Reserve to recover.

Nations can join and form a common law for OTC derivatives to reduce legal and regulatory uncertainty.

Disclosures is the form of making OTC derivative on balance sheet from off Balance Sheet, for which trend is there in the form of derivative disclosure standard in FAS 133 in US. Making OTC trading electronic (instead of using fax, telephone and telex) and making information sharing about counter party risk more formal and structured will go to reduce the risk by making it more transparent.

Systemic risk can be improved by prescribing capital adequacy on off balance sheet exposure and finding out various ways by which off balance sheet exposure can be quantified. Marking to market these exposures will prevent accumulation of undisclosed losses for long periods.

In a globalized economy where world is getting increasingly integrated, any nation pursuing independent monetary policy is not possible. As evidenced by interest rate policy followed by UK, as a consequence of high interest rate policy followed by Bundens Bank, led to George Soros attack on Pound, same kind of lesson was taught by crisis in South East Asia. The message is that increasingly world over the Central banks should follow a policy of price stability rather than multiple objectives.

Increasing integration of global capital market leads to spill over as evidenced by the effect of NASDAQ and NYSE fall in September immediately getting reflected in BSE and NSE, thus nation should increasingly coordinate to stabilize international financial system.

Derivatives unbundles the risk from transactions and facilitates price discovery. Derivatives have high leverage so they generate high profits in good time but on the downside, it can burn the capital in the downside. For example if a share is purchased for Rs.200 and after one month it becomes Rs. 210 or Rs. 190, then the resultant profit or loss is 60%. The margin trading is done where the margin needed is 10%, if a person has Rs. 20,00,000 he can purchase 20,000 shares or if he does Margin trading he can purchase two lacks shares. If the share price rises to Rs. 210 his profit will be 1200 %, while if the share price becomes Rs. 190 he loses the entire capital. Because of the risky nature of derivatives top management should clearly lay down policies about the limits of trading in various derivatives, reporting requirements, and whether trading in derivative will be treated as cost or profit centers. A suitable balancing should be done between risk and control to manage risk like in any other business function. If that is not done, there is little point in blaming derivatives for losses.

7.7 FORWARD COVER

Forward Cover is an OTC contract and here the rate is fixed between two counter parties for taking the underlying currency at a particular date at a predetermined rate. In option forward contract, delivery can be taken during any date in a given month of delivery. For example a second month forward can be taken delivery any time during the end beginning of the second month to end of second month. Date of delivery of the Forward contact is two days after the end of the month of delivery. Since option forward contact gives option to take delivery any time during a month, most of the adverse rate during this period is passed on to the constituency. Since the liquidity of the forward contract depends on the ability to predict the movement of the currency, long dated forward contracts are always less liquid compared to short dated forward contracts. A loan involving repayment over a long period can be hedged using roll over forward contacts, which even though do not act as perfect hedge gives partial protection against adverse rate movement. Forward cover can be settled through delivery, cancellation, extension and early delivery. Banks usually act as intermediaries and charge a commission for the same.

In India forward contracts can be used only for hedging and not for speculative purpose. Thus, the authorized dealer is required to verify the contract before booking forward cover. Further to discourage speculation as per RBI regulations, cancellation of forward contract should be done at the reverse TT rate whatever may be the actual loss or gain to the authorized dealer. Thus, the bank makes more profits by cancelling a contract than by delivering the same.

Forward contract for delivery in earlier months is always more liquid than forward contracts for delivery in later months. This is because forward contract is nothing but expectation about futures; longer the period of future less is the ability to predict the same, due to which trading and liquidity decreases while as a consequence premium increases.

Forward contract cannot be said to be a perfect forecast of future exchange rates since forward rate takes into consideration all present news and expected changes in futures, but a risk premium is added for unexpected changes which may be more or less.

Swap points can be at premium or at discount.

7.8 EXAMPLES

1. An exporter sells a 30 day bill, 2 months from now drawn on a Japanese importer for 50,00,000 Japanese Yen. The interbank rates are as follows.

   (Rs/ 100 Japanese Yen) = 27.20 per 100 yen.

   2 months premium = 20 paise

   3 months premium = 30 paise

   4 months premium = 40 paise

   Transit period is 15 days. Compute the rate.

   Two months from now one month sight bill will be drawn which will be accepted after 15 days being the transit period forward rate is 4th month option that is most adverse rate to exporter from end of third month to end of fourth month which in this case is 27.50 per hundred yen.

2. Electronic Corporation Ltd, customer has imported 5000 cartridges at a landed cost in Bombay, of US$ 20 each. They have the choice of paying for the goods immediately or in three months time. They

have an overdraft limit with SBI Mumbai where 18% P.A. interest rate is charged. Calculate which of the following method will be cheaper to Electronic Corporation.

a. Pay in three months time with interest at 15% and cover the exchange risk forward for three months.

b. Settle now at the spot rate and pay interest on overdraft for three months.

The rates are:

Bombay Rs/$ spot = 46/46.50

3 months swap = 25/35.

Ignore commission.

Even though the forward quotes are not given as premium or discount it can be taken as premium since swap is quoted in ascending order.

So third month forward rate = 46.25/ 46.85.

If option a is chosen total amount to be paid

1,00, 000$ and 15% Interest at the end of three months =1,03,750 $

Forward rate is 46.85 so total rupee payment liability is = Rs. 48,60,688

If the amount is immediately paid liability = Rs. 46,50,000

Three months interest rate at 18% is = 2,09,250

Total liability is = Rs. 48,59,250

Thus option b is better.

3. An importer has booked forward contract for purchase of 1,00,000 USD at Rs. 48 two months from now. At the end of first month he wants to cancel the contract. First month forward rate quoted at the end of first month is 47.75/48. What will be the liability of importer? Ignore commission.

If at the end of first month the importer wants to cancel the contract the bank will have to take delivery and instead of selling to the importer sells it in the market at 47.75. The difference of .25 Rs per dollar is passed on to the importer as cancellation charges at Rs 25,000.

4. In the above problem at the end of the period importer wants to extend the contract for a month. Spot rate at the End of the period is 48.25/48.50 and first month swap is 25/30, how the transaction will be effected if commissions are ignored?

The forward contract will be cancelled at the near end leg and gain made (48.25- 48) will be passed on to the importer. The contract will be rebooked for first month at 48.80.

5. Suppose an importer has booked second month forward for Rs 48 for 1,00,000 $ and at the end of one month wants delivery of dollar if spot rate at the end of first month is 47.50/47.75 and first month forward is 20/25, what are charges to importer or gain to importer through early delivery. Assume RBI regulated interest rate for swap is 12% p.a.

   He will purchase dollar at 47.75 and sell to importer for 48 thus there will be a positive gain of (48-47.75) to the dealer per dollar or Rs 25,000 for 1,00,000$ which he will pay interest at 12% for one month that is Rs 250.

   First month premium of .25 paise per dollar will be passed on to importer that is Rs. 25,000. Thus net cost to importer is (25,000–250) = 24750 Rs ignoring commission.

6. An importer has entered into a loan for 15,00,000 $ for 2 years payable in two equal annual installments the exchange rate structures are given below.

   Spot: 48/48.50

   Sixth Month Forward: 50/ 51

   After Six months

   Spot: 51/52

   Sixth month forward: 53/54

   After one year

   Spot: 55/56

   Sixth month forward: 56/57

   After 18 months

   Spot: 58/59

   Sixth month forward: 60/61

   After 24 months

   Spot: 62/63

   The loan taker can enter into 6 months roll over contract. At the end of first six months he can take delivery of 15,00,000 $ at Rs. 51/$ and sell the same at Rs. 51 thus making no loss or gain. At the end of six months he can again rebook forward contract for six months at 54. He can remit 7,50,000$ at Rs. 54 per dollar instead of spot rate of Rs. 56 and sell the Balance 7,50,000 $ at Rs. 55 and make a profit of Rs. 7,50,000.

For 7,50,000 the contract will be rolled over for another six months at Rs. 57. After 18 months he can take delivery of 7,50,000$ at 57 and sell at Rs. 58. and make a profit of Rs. 7,50,000. The contract will be rolled over for further six months at Rs. 61.

At the end of 24 months balance 7,50,000$ will be remitted at Rs. 61 instead of spot rate of Rs. 63.

The in-between profits can be reinvested and the proceeds from reinvestment can also be used to partially hedge the loan.

Merchants and dealers in foreign exchange are principle users of forward market.

7. An Indian exporter has exposure in Euro. Amount to be paid after 3 months. The three months forecasted exchange rate and Forward rate are given below. Give suggestion whether the exporter should hedge through Forward market or not?

Spot Rs/$ 45.5/46

3 month forward swap 50/60

Exposure in Euro is 1,00,000 Euro

Spot $/ Euro 1.1/ 1.2

3 month swap .1/.15

3 month expected Rs/$ rate is 45.75/ 46.25

3 month expected $/ Euro rate is 1.3/1.4

Since the Swap point is in ascending order the quote is in premium for $ against rupee.

3 month quote Rs/$ = 46/46.6

Same is the case in $/ Euro where third month quote is

$/ Euro = 1.2/ 1.35

Third month Rupee/ Euro Forward rate is = Rs/$* $/Euro

= 46* 1.2/ 46.6* 1.35

= 55.2/ 62.91

3 month expected Rs/ Euro rate = Rs/$* $/ Euro

= 45.75* 1.3/ 46.25* 1.4

= 59.48/ 64.75

Thus the Indian exporter if he leaves his hedge uncovered will receive Rs 59.48 rather than Rs. 55.2 if he leaves it covered. So an uncovered position is appropriate. But Foreign Exchange Market being efficient market predicting accurately is not possible, so a partial hedge say up to 25% is desirable.

8. If an importer has to pays 1,00,000$ after three months and the spot Rupee $ rate is Rs/ $ = 46/46.5

   3 month forward is 40/ 30

   India rate of interest is = 12/13 while the US interest rate is 5%/ 6%. Whether Money Market or Forward market hedge is desirable.

   3 month Dollar is in discount since the swap quote is in descending order.

   3 month Rupee $ quote is = 45.6/ 46.2

   Interest for 3 months investment is 5% per annum. In $ market so amount to be invested in $ to get 1,00,000$ after 3 months is = 100000/(1.0125)

   = 98765$

   Amount to be paid for borrowing 98765$ = 98765 * 46.5

   = Rs. 4592573

   3 months later payment of borrowings = 4592573 * (1.0325)

   = Rs. 4741832

   Thus if payment is made through Forward Market it is Rs. 46,20,000 and it is cheaper.

9. If the Spot rate of $ = 46.5 / 47. If the Indian rate of interest is 13/ 14 and the amount of export proceeds to be received after 3 months is 1,00,000 what is the $ rate of interest for which the exporter will be indifferent between money and forward market. If the Forward swap is 25/30.

   Let us assume rate of borrowing in US $ I

   (1,00000/(1+i/4))* 46.5*(1.13/4) = 1,00,000* 46.75

   48,01,000/(1+ i/4) = 46,75,000

   1+ i/4 = 4801000/ 4675000 = 1.0270

   i/4 = .0270

   I = .0270* 4 = .1080

   If US borrowing rate is 10.8% the company can be indifferent between Forward and money market hedge.

10. If Rs/$ spot rate is 46/46.5

$ / Euro spot is = 1.05/1.1

3 month forward Rs / $ = 25/30

3 month $/ Euro = 3 /2

The exporter has the option of either billing 1,00,000 Euro or choosing $ at the present spot rate. Which option should the exporter follow?

Present $ billing for equivalent to 1,00,000 Euro = 1,00,000* 1.05

= 1,05,000 $

After 3 months realisation if forward rate is booked is = 1,05,000* 46.25

= 48,56,250 Rs.

If billing is done in Euro

3 month Rs/ Euro rate = Rs/ $ * $/ Euro

= 46.25* 1.02 / 46.8* 1.08

= 47.18/ 50.54

By billing in Euro he gets 1,00,000* 47.18 = Rs.47,18.000

Thus, billing in $ is better.

7.9 FUTURES

Futures are exchange traded instruments. Clearing house of the exchange, act as a counter party in each transaction. Since clearing houses are well capitalized entities they also protect themselves by imposing initial margin based on VAR and maintenance margin, which constitute 75% of initial margin and daily variation margin known as marking to market.

VAR* means Value at Risk where 68.4% constitute Mean$\pm$ 1 Standard Deviation, 95.5% constitute $\pm$ 2Standard Deviation, 99.7% constitute $\pm$ 3Standard Deviation. Based on this range of fluctuation is determined by past data since normal distribution involves smooth

* Full form in Glossary

continuous change. Margins are taken both from seller and buyer. Since VAR does not factor in event risk, models are built taking into consideration event risk and this model building process is known as risk metrics. When the margin level falls below maintenance margin, then the margin call is made to make it equal to initial margin.

Since there are no counter party risks in Futures, it acts as an efficient instrument for price discovery. Even though cost of carry of underlying in the form of interest rate, storage cost and dividend, the price of future cannot be determined by cost of carry alone and this is known as *Convenience Yield.* Futures are more liquid compared to forward, futures do not have counter party risk as compared to forward, future calls for margins while there is no need for margins in forward, future facilitate price discovery due to absence of counter party risk, same is not the case with forward, futures are standard in delivery, size etc. while forwards are customized. Minimum price changes which will be recognized in future contract is called as *Tick Size.*

Important trading of futures takes place in Chicago Board of Trade, London International Financial Future Exchange, Tokyo International Financial Future Exchange, and Singapore International Financial Future Exchange, Swiss Options and Financial Future Exchange, Sydney Future Exchange. Future being standard product is not a perfect hedge. In Future, exchange price risk is the only risk that is hedgeable. Futures are used extensively for sophisticated hedging like *beta hedging* and *portfolio insurance.* Interest Rate risk can also be hedged by using interest rate futures.

7.10 EXAMPLES

1. Gold future for a particular Day was quoting at 500$ per ounce and minimum size of the contract is 100 ounce. If the initial margin is fixed as 2000$ and maintenance margin as 1500$, show the movement in margin account for next five days assuming the next five days price of future contract as 498$, 490$, 470$, 510$, 500$. Assume Margins in excess of initial margin are not withdrawn.

Buyer		Cumulative Margin
Initial Margin	2000$	
Day 1 Margin	(200$)	1800$
Day 2 Margin	(800$)	1,000$(Margin call of 1000$)
Day 3 Margin	(2000$)	0 (Margin call of 2000$)
Day 4 Margin	4000$	6000$
Day 5 Margin	(1000$)	5000$
Seller		
Initial Margin	2000$	
Day 1 Margin	200$	2200$
Day 2 Margin	800$	3000$
Day 3 Margin	2000$	5000$
Day 4 Margin	(4000)	1000$ (Margin call 1000$)
Day 5 Margin	1000$	3000$

2. If an importer in US has payables of 100000 pound sterling to be made three months from now. Present rate of $/Pound sterling is 1.71/1.72/PS. If three months future contracts are quoted at 1.76$/PS. If he expects the dollar to depreciate what action should he take assuming dollar actually depreciated after three months to 1.77$/PS. Present Future contract is quoting at 1.76$ /PS after three months future contract quotes at 1.80$/PS. Since the future contract expires on the end of the three months while payment has to be made at the beginning of third month. Future contracts are traded in minimum size of 62,500 PS. What action to be taken by importer for hedging the exporter.

Since futures are coming in standard size and standard delivery date the date of delivery and size do not match.

He can buy 2 future contracts of pound for third month delivery. After three months if $ depreciates to 1.76/PS loss to the exporter is (1,00,000 PS * .05$) = 5000$. While gain in future market is (1,25,000 PS* .04$) = 5000$. Thus, Futures act as perfect hedge in this case which may not always be so.

a) In the above problem if an exporter in UK has to receive $ after three months what hedging he will do.

He will sell third month dollar future to hedge himself.

b) If a Forex dealer expects the dollar to deprecia In March 2003 September Future is Rs. 49. What strategy he can adopt to take care of his prediction if standard size of Future contract is 1,00,000$.

He can sell one Standard Future contract for September. Suppose in July the prediction turns out to be true and actual rate of future for delivery in September is Rs.48 then he can buy one Future contract for delivery in September and deliver against the other contract, making a profit of Rs. 1 per $ and profit Rs.1,00,000.

3. A person in UK is planning to import an equipment of 2,00,0000 $. Spot rate as of now is pound = 1.72 $. December Future is trading at 1.68$, he expects pound to depreciate further against $. Standard Future contract is 1,25,000 PS, what action he can take to hedge his position.

Amount of Pound Sterling liability = 2000000/ 1.72

= 11, 62,791 PS.

No. of future contract = 1162791/ 125000

= 9.3

= 9 future contract

He can sell 9 future contract of PS for Delivery in December at PS= 1.68$.

In December if the Actual spot $/ PS = 1. 65

While December future is quoted at 1.64$. What is the loss to the importer?

Loss in Spot Market = 2000000/1.72- 2000000/1.65

= 1162791- 1212121= 49330$

Gain in Future Market

Buy 9 Future contract for December delivery for = 125000* 9* 1.64$ = 1845000 $

Deliver against December sold contract at 1.68$ and make again of 9* 125000* 1.68= 1890000$

Make a net gain of 45,000$ thereby limiting the $ loss to 4330$.

4. If the spot Rs/ $ contract is 47/ 47.5 interest rate for 3 months period for $ 6/6.5%, while for Rs it is 12/12.5% 3 month Future contract is selling at Rs.49 and standard size of a $ contract is 1,00,000. What opportunity exists for Arbitrage?

Borrow 1$ at 6.5% convert it in to Rupee at 47 and invest for 3 months in Rupees at 12%.

Three months later

1.01625$ = 47* 1.03

1.01625$ = 48.41

$ = 48.41/ 1.01625 = 47.64 Rs.

Thus, the Future contract is overvalued.

Sell one standard future contract at Rs.49.

Borrow Rs. 98522* 47.5 = Rs. 4679795 at 12.5% and invest in $ so that after 3 months 1,00,000$ will be received.

After three months Amount to be paid in Rupee is 4679795 * 1.03125 = Rs. 4826039

By delivering 1,00,000$ against future contact one can get Rs. 49,00,000

Arbitrage is = 49,00,000- 48,26,039

= Rs. 73961 Profit.

5. If the Spot $ / PS rate is 1.71 a trader expects $ to further depreciate against pound 3 month future is trading at $ 1.73, 6 month future is trading at $ 1.77, standard size of future contract for Pound Sterling is 62,500 PS What will happen, if the trader employs spread trading or if he does not employ spread trading if three months latter $ 1.75/ Pound? After three months 3rd month Pound Sterling future trades at $ 1.80. If three months latter Pound Sterling trades at $ 1.70 and 3rd month future trades at $ 1.67 what will be the result if spread trading is employed or not employed?

In the first case if he decides to employ spread trading he will buy six months pound future and sell 3 months pound future then his gain will be,

6 months futures = 62500* (1.80–1.77)

= 62500* .03

= $ 1875

Loss in three months contract will be = 62500(1.73–1.75)

= 62500* .02

= $ 1250

Net gains will be = 1875–1250

= $ 625.

If he has not employed spread trading his gain will be 1875$.

In the second case.

Loss if he employs spread trading is

6 months

62500*(1.77–1.67) = $ 6250

Gain in 3months

62500 *(1.73–1.70) = $ 1875

Net loss will be = 6250–1875

= $ 4375

If he has not employed spread trading loss will be $ 6250.

Thus, spread trading is a risk reduction device. Like all risk reduction devices, it not only reduces losses but also limits profits.

6. If a corporate is going to receive 1 million $ 3 months from now. It can invest this amount in 6 months treasury bill. Present rate is 8% for 6 months deposit but the corporate fears that three months later interest rate will fall. It hedges the position by buying interest rate future for delivery 6 months later. Per base point the value is 50$. Suppose if fears turn true 3 months later the treasury interest rate for 6 months falls to 7.25% what will be its loss?

   It's loss due to fall in interest rate = 10,00,000* .75/2= 1000000* .0375

   = $ 3750.

   He can hedge the same by buying 10 futures

   (92.75–92) * 100* $ 50 = $ 3750

   Thus, Buying interest rate future acts as perfect hedge.

7. If an Indian corporate has to pay 1 million pounds 3 months later it expects pound to appreciate against rupee. But there is no Future contract of Rupee against Pound. So decides to hedge the same through $ futures against pound.

   If Rs /$ = 46.75/47

   $/ Pound = 1.71/1.73

   Rs/ Pound = 46.75* 1.71/ 47* 1.73

   = 79.94/ 81.31

3rd month future $/ pound = 1.75$

Standard pound future contract size = 1,25,000 pounds.

Buy 8 pound future contract.

If three months later

Rs/ $ = 47.5/ 48

$/ pound = 1.77/ 1.78

Three month rate Rs/ pound = 47.5* 1.77/ 48* 1.78

= 84.08/ 85.44

3 Month pound future contract is 1.78$

Loss due to 3 month payment = (85.44-81.31) * 10,00,000= 41,30,000Rs

In $ term gain in future contract = 30,000$

In terms of rupee gain = 30,000* 47.5= Rs. 14,25,000

Thus, Future acts as partial hedge.

8. If a corporate wants to borrow 1 million $ 3 months from now for a period of 3 months present rate is 7.5% and he expects the interest rate to increase he can hedge against this by selling ten interest rate futures of 1,00,000$ each at 92.5 per base point 25$, actual interest rate for three months turns out to be 8% calculate the loss.

Hedge due to interest rate = 10,00,000* .5/ 4= 5000/4= 1,250$

Gain due to interest rate future = 25$ .5* 100= 1,250

Thus interest rate future acts as perfect hedge.

9. A future contract is available for petrol at 28$ per barrel. Each contract is for 1,00,000 barrel. You have contracted for 8 long futures. The contract is entered into on 15th June 2003, and expires on June 30 2003. The initial margin is 10% of the contract value and maintenance margin is 75% of the initial margin. You have to prepare a statement of marking to market showing.

Daily loss gain 2. Margin account balance 3. Margin call.

The closing $ prices of petrol per barrel in the spot market on various days are as follows.

Date	Initial Margin	Margin Debit	Margin Credit	Total Margin
	2,80,000			
June16 (28.50)			4,00,000	6,80,000
June 17 (31)			2000000	2680000
June 18 (33)			1600000	4280000
June20 (28.25)		38,00,000		4,80,000
June21 (27.55)		5,60,000	Margin Call 3,60,000	(80,000)
June22 (26.50)		8,40,000	Margin Call 8,40,000	2,80,000
June23 (26.45)		40,000	Margin Call 40,000	2,80,000
June24 (26.10)		2,80,000	Margin Call 2,80,000	2,80,000

7.11 OPTION

Option means right without obligation. Since it involves such flexibility premium has to be paid upfront. The players involved in option market are *option writer* and *option holder*. Option is both OTC as well as exchange traded instruments. Option holder's maximum loss is option premium, while option writer's maximum loss is without limits. When there is significant uncertainty in the direction of movement, underlying options are used.

Options can be classified as *call* and *put* option.

Call option is a right without obligation to buy, while put option is right without obligation to sell an underlying at a future date which is known as option period at a particular price called *strike price* or *exercise price*.

European option can be exercised only at the end of option period, while American option can be exercised any time during the option period. Since American option involves extra flexibility, it involves higher premium.

In the case of call option if the spot price is more than the exercise price, the option is said to be in the money. If spot price is equal to the exercise price, the option is said to be at the money and if the spot price is less than exercise price, it is said to be out of the money. Vice versa is true for put option.

The factors, which determine the value of the option are?

7.11.1 Price of the Underlying

The relationship between the price of the underlying and price of the option is called as *Delta*. Delta of call option can be between 0 and + 1, while delta of put option will be between 0 and –1.

7.11.2 Time Period

Longer the time period greater will be the value of the option. Relationship between time period and value of the option is called as *Theta*. Theta is also called as time decay of the option

7.11.3 Interest Rate

Higher the interest rate, greater the value of call option and vice versa is true for put option. The relationship between interest rate and price of the option is called as *Rho*. This is due to the fact if the interest rate is high then the investor would prefer to hold call option and invest the balance money to earn attractive returns. Thus, increase in demand will cause the value of the option to rise. Vice versa will be true for put option.

7.11.4 Volatility

Higher the volatility of underlying, greater will be the value of the option. The relationship between the volatility of the underlying and value of option is called as *vega*, *lamda* or *kappa*. Because the option writer will like to write option on low volatile underlying due to predictability of the price, the option holder would like to purchase option only on assets which are highly volatile. Thus higher the volatility, more will the value of both call and put options.

If the underlying is a dividend paying stock, greater the chance of getting a dividend lower will be the value of call option; this is due to the fact dividend received will reduce the premium.

The difference between spot price and strike price of an option is called as *intrinsic value*. Difference between intrinsic value and option premium is called as time value.

There are various types of exotic options:

1. *Boston option:* Here the premium is paid at the end of the option period instead of beginning.
2. *Bermuda option:* Here premium is paid in periodic intervals instead of beginning.
3. *Chooser option:* Here at the end of the period one can choose whether he wants a call option or put option.
4. *Look Back option:* Here the spot price is determined based on the price prevailing during option period at the end of option period.
5. *Asian option:* In Asian option spot price is determined based on the average price of underlying during option period.
6. *Binary option or lottery:* Here once the spot price exceeds option price in the case of call option the payoff will be several multiples.
7. *Knockin option:* In knockin option once the price of underlying reaches particular level the option gets locked in.
8. *Knockout option:* Here once the price of underlying reaches a particular level the option holder will not be eligible to claim any further benefit.
9. *Qanto:* Here the settlement is made in a currency different from that of underlying currency.
10. *Rainbow option:* Here the underlying is multiple instead of single.

11. *Swaption:* Here the underlying of an option itself is in the form of another derivative like swap or cap or a floor.

There are various trading strategies of options like Straddles, Strangles, Strips, Straps and Spread trading. There are two methods of valuing options and they are *Binomial* and *Black Scholes*.

In binomial model the future price is assumed to take only two values one is the upper limit and other one is a lower limit. The price of the call option can be measured by using the following formulae:

Price of call option = CuP+Cd(1-p)/R

Where U is the upper range of stock price, d is lower range of stock price, P= R-d/u-d

R= 1+r where r is risk free interest rate.

Price of the put option can be measured by using the following formulae:

Price of put option = PuP+Pd(1-P)/R

Under *Black Scholes* model

Price of call option is = S N(d1) – Xe^rt N(d2)

D1= In S/X+ (r+(sigma)^2)t/sigma* Squate root of t.

D2 = d1 – sigma* square root of t.

Where S is spot price of underlying, N(d1) is standard normal distribution, X is exercise price of option, r is risk free interest rate e = 2.718, t is time period in year, Sigma is std deviation of the underlying tracked on a continuous basis. In other words Black Scholes model says that the price of call option is spot price less exercise price discounted at continuous compounded rate.

Black Scholes model assumes perfect market with no transaction cost, no taxes, log normal distribution, valid only for European option. In spite of these limitations, the model works well in practice.

Value of put option = Xe^rtN(-d2)- SN(-d1).

Interest rate can be hedged by using cap or collar which is used for fixing upper and lower limits.

The basic model is about the spot value multiplied by the risk and exercise price discounted at continuously compounded interest rate instead of the normal interest rate log normal distribution since the upside potential for a call option for the call option holder is unlimited while downside is limited, thus log normal distribution is more appropriate than normal distribution. Limitations of this model are that no transaction cost or tax is assumed. In spite of all these difficulties, Black Scholes model works in practice.

An Option is considered as zero sum game since the gain to option writer is an equivalent loss to option holder and vice versa.

7.12 EXAMPLES

1. German Firm buys a call option on $ 10,00,000 with a strike price of DM 1.60/$ and a premium of DM .03/$. The interest Rate opportunity cost is 6% per annum. Maturity period is 180 days.

a) What is the Break even Spot rate beyond which the firm makes a net gain.

b) Suppose the six month forward rate at the time of option was 1.62DM/$

What is the range of maturity spot rate for which the option will prove better than forward rate? Year can be taken as 360 days for this purpose.

Upfront Premium .03DM at 6% interest rate .03*.06*180/360 = .009 DM thus total premium for option is .039 DM So for any spot rate below (1.62-.039) = 1.581DM option will be better than Forward.

2. If a dealer acquires a call option to purchase 1,00,000$, for Rs. 47 deliverable after one month by paying a premium of .10 paise per $. Construct a pay off table if the price of rupee against $ is 46, 48, 49, 47, 45

Pay off Table

Rs. 46 option will not be exercised and the premium of Rs. 10,000 will be loss.

Rs. 48 pay off will be (48–47–0.10) * 100000$ = Rs. 90,000

Rs. 49 payoff will be (49–47–0.10) * 100000$ = 1,90,000

At Rs. 47 since the value of the option and underlying price is same loss will be equal to premium Rs. 10,000.

At 45 since the underlying price is less than the exercise price option will not be exercised and the loss will be Rs. 10,000.

3. What is the payoff for put option?

Rs. 46 put option will be exercised. The payoff (1,00,000$)* (47-46) – 10,000(premium)= 90,000Rs

Rs.48 put option will not be exercised and the loss will be premium of Rs 10,000.

Rs. 49 put option will not be exercised and the loss will be Rs.10,000

Rs. 49 again the put option will not be exercised then the loss will be Rs 10,000.

Rs 45 put option will be exercised (100000$)* (47–45)–10,000 = Rs. 1,90,000

4. A call option has been entered for delivery of 1$ at Rs. 46 if it is predicted that the probability of future price is

.20	47
.25	45
.35	48
.15	50
.05	49

What premium the purchaser of option will break even?

Let the premium be P

P = (47–46–P) * .20 + (–P) * .25 + (48–46–P) * .35+ (50–46–P) *.15+ (49–46–P)*.05

0 = .20– .20 P–.25P+ .7–.35P+ .6–.15P +.15– .05P

= 1.65 –1P

P = 1.65 Rs.

5. If the price of $ = 47 Rs as of now, if the upper range is 1.2 and lower range is .8 what is the price of call option if the exercise price is under single stage binomial model if the risk free rate of interest is 6%.

Price of call option= Cu P + Cd (1–P)

R

P = R–D/U–D

= 1.06–.8/ 1.2-.8

= .26/ .4

= .65

= 47* .2*.65 + 0/ (1.06)

= 9.4 *.65/ (1.06)

= 6.11/ (1.06)

= 5.76

6. In the above case what is the value of put option.

Premium for put option = Pu* p + Pd * (1–p)/R

= 9.4 * .35+ 0/ (1.06)

= 3.11

7. In the above problem, if it is a two stage binomial value, is it better to exercise the option as European option or American option?

Rs 14.09

47 ------------------------------ 56.4-----------.65---------- 67.68

| .65 | |

96

| .35 |

| 0 | | .35

37.6 ---.65---- 45.12 45.12

|

| .35

30.08

Call option value at the first node

= Cu* p+ cd (1–p)/(1.06)

= 21.68* .65+ 0/(1.06)

= 14.09

Thus the value today is 14.09*.65/1.06 = 8.64

Value at the second node is = 47* .2* .65+ 0/(1.06)

= 6.11/ (1.06)

= 5.76 Rs

Thus it is better to exercise it as European than American option.

8. If the spot price of an asset is 45 exercise price is Rs.50 exercise period is 3 months, standard deviation is 20%, risk free rate is 6% what is the value of call and put option under Black Scholes model?

   Value of call option = S* N (d1) – Xe^–rt N (d2)

   D1 = In S/E +(r+ (sigma) ^2/2)*t/ sigma *square root t

   D2 = d1 – sigma * square root of t.

   D1 = In 45/50+(.06+ (.20)^2/2) * .25/ .2*

   = + (.06+.02)* .25/.2* .5

   = –.1053 + .02/(.1)

   = –.0853/.1= . –.853

   D2 = –.853 – .20* .5

   = –.853–.1

   = –.953

   N(d1) = .1968

   N(d2) = .1703

   C = 45 * .1968 – 50* (2.718) ^ –.06* .25 * .1703

   = 8.856 – 50*.9852* .1703

   = 8.856–8.389

   = .467 Rs

   Value of put option

   C = X e^–rt* N(d2)–S N(–d1)

   = 50* .9852* .9857 – 45*.8032

   = 48.56–36.14

   = 12.42 Rs.

9. What is the delta, gamma, Theta, Vega and Rho for the above problem?

   1. Delta : .1968

      N (d1) is Delta.

   2. Gamma = N'(d1)/ S* SIGMA* Square root of T.

      N'(d1) = e^–.5*(d1)^2./ Square root of 2 Pi

      = e ^-..5(–.853) ^2/ 45* .20* .5

      = 1/ 1.4387* 1.7728

      = .3921

= .3921/ 4.5

Gamma = .087

Theta = –S* N' (d1) * Sigma/ 2*Square root of T – Risk free interest rate * Exercise price* e ^–Rt* N (d2).

= –45* .3921*.20/2*.5 – .06* 50 * .1703/1.0618

= –3.5289 – .4812

= –4.0101

Vega = S* Square root of T* N' (d1)

= 45* .5* .3921

= 8.82

Rho = X * T* e^–Rt* N (d2)

= 50* .25 * .1703/ (1.015)

= 2.0972

10. A Speculator is considering the purchase of five three months Japanese Yen call options with strike price of 96 cent per 100 Yen. The premium is 1.35 cents per 100 Yen. The spot price is 95.28 cents per 100 yen and the 90 days forward rate is 95.71 cents. The speculators believe that the yen will appreciate to 1$ per 100 yen over the next three months. As the speculator's assistant, you have been asked to do the following.

1. Indicate pay off matrix for call option.
2. Determine the speculator's profit if yen appreciates to 1$/100 yen.
3. Determine the speculator's profit if yen appreciates only to forward rate.
4. Determine the future spot price at which the speculator only breaks even.

1. If yen is definitely going to appreciate forward is better than option. Option will be profitable, if the $ appreciates to 94.36 or at a figure more than that.
2. If Yen appreciates to 1$ speculator's profit is 4–1.35 = 2.65 yen per contract and for 5 contracts it is 5* 2.65 = 13.25 cents.
3. If yen appreciates only to Forward rate then the loss will be 1.35* 5 = 6.75 yen that is the premium paid since the speculator will never exercise the call option.

4. Future spot price at which speculator will break even is 97.35 cents for 100 yen.

7.13 SWAP

Swap means exchange, which involves exchange of stream of currencies or interest rate either between fixed and floating rate of interest. Floating rate of interest involves different basis like treasury and *Libor* which involves a basis swap. Swap is based on Ricardo's theory of comparative advantage. Sometimes spread of borrowing between fixed and floating occurs due to *Quality Spread Differential*. Quality Spread differential occurs due to credit rating difference due to which fixed interest loan whose interest cannot be repriced during the tenor of the loan carries a higher spread depending on credit rating of borrower, compared to a floating rate interest loan.

Apart from this, currency swap occurs due to perception in market like the US market has low tolerance for financial leverage while Japanese market has high tolerance level. Similarly, repeated borrowing in a particular market leads to saturation effect like in the case of first swap concluded between IBM and World Bank wherein IBM borrowed in Switzerland and World Bank borrowed in US due to saturation effect of repeated borrowings by IBM in US Market. Swap market began due to exchange control regulations in many European countries including UK till late seventies. Suppose a company in UK wanted to give loan to its subsidiary in USA, it was not able to do so due to exchange control regulations. It found out another company in US which wanted to lend to its subsidiary in UK in Pound Sterling to swap the loan amount. Thus, the UK Company could lend in Pound Sterling to US subsidiary and US parents lent equivalent amount to UK subsidiary in US $. But the problem arose because the method of swapping in the event of US subsidiary of UK parent defaulting in its loan. It could not be legally offset against the borrowing of US subsidiary from UK parent.

Swap is an OTC market. Currency Swap can be treated as a series of forward contracts used for hedging long term exposures. Banks had warehoused swaps and sold them off the shelf and took position and hedged their exchange risk thereby standardizing the instruments and avoiding costly search for counter party for each transaction. Today, Swap documents are standardized throughout the world by International Swap Dealers Association (ISDA). Parties can cover their interest rate risk by taking or writing a Forward Rate Agreement (FRA).

Thus, from mid eighties onwards, Swaps are standardized by ISDA and just traded like an Exchange Traded Instrument. The bank takes a position which automatically acts as a hedge against interest rate as well as exchange risk undertaken by the bank.

Previously, an International bank would be hesitant to lend or borrow in a currency of the country where the bank had no natural hedge because of the risk of adverse movement of exchange rate. Now currency swap can be used to cover the same.

Similarly, the possibility of matching borrowing through fixed rate and lending in variable rate or vice versa can be largely covered through *interest rate swap*. A currency swap is considered as series of forward cover transactions.

Swap has two counter party risks, for example in a currency swap both the parties act as both lender and borrower thereby enhancing the risk element of a swap.

Forward rate agreements are betting on future interest rates. They are so called due to the danger of same being declared as illegal due to wagering laws.

7.13.1 Swap a Practical Illustration

Suppose IDBI needs $ funds. If it approaches US market it will get the same at Libor + 4%, while HDFC being a Housing Finance Institution approaches US market then it will get the funds at Libor + .25%. If IDBI approaches Indian market it will get funds at 14% while HDFC approaches Indian Market it will get funds at 12% then even though HDFC has absolute advantage of borrowing in both the markets it has comparative advantage in borrowing in US market while IDBI has comparative advantage in borrowing in Indian market. The QSD or Quality Spread Differential is 3.75–2 = 1.75.

This would have arisen due to the Government patronage enjoyed by both the institutions in India.

A Swap can be arranged by way of sharing of QSD 1.5% to HDFC and .25% to IDBI

HDFC can borrow in US market at Libor + .25% and pass it on to IDBI at Libor + 1.75%, while IDBI can borrow in Indian Market at 14% and pass it on to HDFC at 12%.

Thus, the benefit to HDFC in the transaction is 1.5%, while the benefit to IDBI in the transaction is.

At Dollar Leg = Libor + 4%– Libor + 1.75%= 2.25%

And the Rupee leg loss is = 12–14 = –2%

Overall gain = 2.25–2 = .25%

7.14 EXAMPLES

1. If two persons A and B can borrow in fixed and floating rate market at the following rates calculate QSD, if QSD is to be equally, design a plain cut and paste interest rate swap.

	Party A	Party B
Fixed Rate	9%	10%
Floating rate	Libor + .25	Libor + .75

Here A has got absolute advantage in fixed and floating rate market. But A has relative advantage in Fixed interest market while B has got comparative advantage in Floating rate market.

QSD: 1–.5= .5%

A will borrow in Fixed interest market at 9% and Swap with B for 9.25%, while B will borrow at Floating interest rate at Libor+.75% and Swap with A for fixed rate for Libor+.25% thus both will get equal share of .25% of QSD.

2. If in the above problem a bank acts as intermediary and the commission charged by the bank is .15%, all other things remaining same how will a cut and paste interest rate Swap be arranged?

Out of QSD of .5% .15% is bank commission and will be reduced out of QSD and balance will be shared equally at .175% between A and B.

A can borrow at 9% in fixed interest market and Swap with B for 9.175, while B can borrow at floating rate market at Libor+.75 and Swap with A for Libor+ .25 and B will pay commission of .15% to bank.

3. The treasurer of an insurance company expects to have a surplus of 5 million pounds 6 months from now. She has decided to park the

funds in a 3 month Euro Sterling deposit. The current 3 month deposit rate is 9%. A 6/9, 5 million pound FRA is being quoted at 8.75/9%. The treasurer sells an FRA to protect herself from falling rates.

Compute the effective rate of interest rate on her investment, if on 182 days, the 3 month deposit rate is 10%.

3 months FRA after 6 months rate is 9%. If the actual rate is 10% then the extra 1% will be paid to the FRA holder thereby locking the effective rate at 9%.

4. If a treasurer of a multinational company want to borrow 1 million $ 3 months from now for a period of six months. Present rate of interest is 9% while the treasurer expects the interest rate to rise. How can he protect himself?

The treasurer can purchase a 6 months FRA for three months from now. If the interest rate rises within 3 months the bank will pay the difference to him but if it falls he has to pay the difference to the bank thereby effectively locking in at 9%.

He can also hedge this by purchasing an interest rate cap. But cap being an option an upfront premium has to be paid. If he is relatively certain that the interest rate will raise he will be better off by purchasing a swap, while he is not certain in which way the interest rate will move but feels that the swing will be huge he will be better off by purchasing an option in the form of cap rather than FRA.

5. A Corporate has swapped 7 year fixed interest rate pound sterling loan of 1million carrying 10% interest rate against $ loan carrying interest rate to be set once in 6 months at 6 months Libor. Exchange rate pound = $ 2. At the time of entering into contract Libor for $ 8%, if 2 years later fixed interest rate on pound has fallen to 9% while variable interest rate Libor on $ has risen to 9% if at that time pound = $ 1.80.

Value of fixed leg contract

6 month	50,000 pounds
1 year	50,000 pounds
18 months	50,000 pounds
24 months	50,000 pounds
30 months	50,000 pounds
36 months	50,000 pounds
42 months	50,000 pounds

48 months	50,000 pounds
54 months	50,000 pounds
60 months	10,50,000 pounds.

Value = PV(50,000, 4.5%, 10) + PV(10,00,000, 9%, 5)

= (1.045)^10–1)/ (1.045)^10* .045= .5530/ .0699

= 7.91* 50000

= 395500

= 649942

= 1045442* 1.80

= 1881796$

20,00,000* (1.04)/ (1.045) = 1990431$

Loss due to swapping = 1990431–1881796

= 108635$

6. Interest rate on Fixed rate is 10%, while that of floating rate is Libor as applicable now is 8%, if the current fixed rate is 11% and floating rate is 9% what is the value of interest rate swap, if the remaining period is 5 years 3 months.

Let the notional principle value be 1 million $

Fixed interest rate

3 months	$ 25,000
9 months	$ 50,000
15 months	$ 50,000
21 months	$ 50,000
27 months	$ 50,000
33 months	$ 50,000
39. months	$ 50,000
45 months	$ 50,000
51 months	$ 50,000
57 months	$ 50,000
63 months	$ 10,50,000

Value = 25000+PVIFA ($ 50,000, 5.5%, 10)+PVIF (10,00,000, 11%, 5)

(1.0275)

= 25,000 + (1.055) ^10– 1/ (1.055)^10* .055) * 50,000+ 10,00,000/(1.11)^5

(1.0275)

= 25,000+18.19* 50000 + 593472

(1.0275)

= 25,000+ 909500 + 593472

(1.0275)

$ 1487077

Value of floating leg = (10,00,000* (1.08/2)/ (1.09/2)

= 995215$

Value of Swap = 1487077– 995215= 491862$

CONCLUSION

In this chapter, we studied how derivatives are used as risk transfer mechanism. We also studied that unless proper controls are laid out by the top management, derivatives can burn the capital and might result in business failures. Various categories of derivatives like exchange traded derivatives and OTC derivatives, difference between them, clearing house mechanism, margin system, VAR for exchange traded derivatives were studied. Individual derivatives like forward, future, options and swap and their trading mechanism were also discussed in detail.

SUGGESTED ASSIGNMENTS

1. Who are principal users of Forward market?
2. Define Option forward.
3. Compare and Contrast forward and Future contract.
4. What is meant by Marking to market?
5. What is meant by Call Option?
6. What is a currency Put Option?
7. When should a firm consider purchase of Call and Put Option for hedging?
8. Define in the money, at the money, out of the money option?
9. What is meant by Quality Spread Differentials?
10. What is meant by Swap transactions?

Chapter 8

An Overview of Global Financial Market

8.1 INTRODUCTION

In 70s borrowing in international market was done only by the Governments or Government-owned entities. Such borrowings were done as a club loan when the quantum of borrowing was relatively small; a group of bankers joined together and financed the same by way of private arrangement. When the volume of loan was huge, a bank acted as lead bank and sold portions of loans to the other banks. Loan syndication was done with multi-currency option. Floating rate of interest was charged. When the syndication arrangement was concluded an advertisement was issued in newspapers announcing conclusion of loan and this agreement was called as *Tombstone advertisement*. The loan contained sovereign immunity waiver clause, which enabled the Government of one country to be sued in another country for the limited purposes of the loan transaction

Euro loans were issued in Euro currencies. They were usually short and medium term in nature. No credit, no withholding taxes on interest, due to absence of reserve requirement rating, were required for the same. The deposit insurance premiums were much cheaper than the regular loans.

8.1.1 Bond Markets

After Euro loans came the *Bond Markets*. Eurobonds were medium term in nature, it was bearer in nature on which interest was paid through coupons, they could be transferred by mere endorsement and delivery, there were no withholding taxes, and they were much cheaper in the absence of several monetary regulations. They were the preferred form of investments for high net worth individuals called as *Belgian Dentists*. Because of these factors Euro Bond market was an easy and convenient market to borrow.

8.1.2 Foreign Currency Bond Markets

Borrowing in US in US dollars by a foreign entity by issuing bond is called as *Yankee Bond*. Borrowing in Japan in Japanese Yen by way of public issue by a non-Japanese entity is called as *Samurai Bond*. Borrowing in Japan in Japanese Yen by way of private placement by a foreign entity is called as *Shibosai Bond*. Borrowing in UK in British Pound by a foreign entity is called as *Bulldog Bond*.

Foreign bonds involve the following:

- registration with regulatory authorities like SEC (Security Exchange Commission),
- disclosure requirement,
- compulsory credit rating, and
- withholding taxes.

In some places like Japan, Q system is also followed. In spite of this system many people go to foreign bond market for their borrowing requirements since they can borrow for long term in foreign bond market, which is not possible in Euro Bond market and markets like US have deep pockets. Various innovations have taken place in bond markets in the form of bonds with call option, put option, convertible bond etc.

8.2 SHORT TERM INSTRUMENTS

Short-term debt instruments are called as *notes.*

8.2.1 Commercial Paper

Commercial paper is rated unsecured instrument with maturity ranging between 6 months to one year. Euro Commercial paper is commercial paper issued in Euro currencies. Euro Commercial Paper is not underwritten. Note issue facilities are unsecured instrument which are underwritten by banks through revolving underwriting facility.

8.2.2 Floating Rate Notes

Floating rate notes (FRNs) are instruments in which interest rate is floating based on bench mark like LIBOR. There are various variants of floating rate notes like floating rate note with multi-currency option, minimax FRN where cap and floor are fixed for interest rates, perpetual FRN which doesn't have any redemption period, flip-flop FRN wherein the holder has an option to treat the FRN as perpetual after holding it for a time period.

Medium Term Notes are facilities issued for more than one year up to desired level of maturity. Insurance companies are the major investors for these funds. Interest rates depend on credit rating, pension funds, banks, mutual funds. These funds do not have any underwriting facility, but of late underwriting facilities are being offered.

8.2.3 Equity Instruments

Depository receipts are equity instruments. They were originally conceived by Morgan and Stanley in 20s to get over US Government regulation prohibiting its pension funds from investing in foreign security. The mechanism of deposit receipts work like this–the issuer issues the security in favour of depository bank, which is usually a foreign bank. Securities are held in by the custodian bank, which is a local bank. Depository bank in turn issues depository receipt, which is a negotiable instrument. It is traded in OTC market as well as is listed in exchange usually Luxembourg and London stock exchanges. Since the investment is not in shares but in deposit receipts they are not considered as foreign security. Depositary receipts are equity and they are two way fungible, that is shares can be converted to deposit receipts and vice versa to avoid inter-market arbitrage. Unlike in the case of loan the investor bears the exchange rate risk and they mandate the depository not to vote. Thus, it becomes equity shares without voting rights.

For issuing GDR, first approval under section 81 has to be taken by way of special resolution from shareholders or by way of ordinary resolution with Central Government approval. Then lead manager has to be appointed. Lead manager plays a crucial role in the success of the issue by way of advising regarding pricing, size and timing of the issue. Lead managers are asked to make presentation which is called as *beauty parade* and on that basis they are selected. For the issue of GDR, Government approval should be taken. Since the international market is highly competitive, it is not possible to determine the price well in advance. The lead manager furnishes the price band to be charged. A path finder prospectus which contains all other details is issued and only for the price, a band is indicated. Investor meets are held in all important centers and are called as *road shows*. Price is determined by book building route wherein the investor himself determines the price.

American Depository Receipt is same but for the fact that those who want to list in American or New York Stock exchange or NASDAQ, have to restate their accounts as per US GAAP(Generally Accepted Accounting Principle) and register themselves with SEC (Security Exchange Commission) and comply with disclosure requirement. Generally, companies with more than 100 million$ of market capitalization can only list in American Stock Exchange. In spite of this, companies go for ADR issues due to the prestige and visibility associated with it and the American markets are very deep.

Securities placed in American market as per regulation 144A or private placement basis need not be listed with stock exchange. They do not need to comply either with US GAAP or SEC disclosure norms.

CONCLUSION

In this chapter, we studied about International Financial Markets like Syndicated Loans, Short term money market instruments, Foreign Bond, Euro Bond Market, Equity Market through DR mechanisms.

SUGGESTED ASSIGNMENTS

1. Define Yankee Bond.
2. What is Floating Rate Note?
3. Explain the characteristics of GDR and how they are priced?
4. Briefly describe the characteristics of Euro Dollar account?
5. List the major advantage of Euro issue to Indian Companies?
6. What are Foreign Bonds?
7. What is meant by MTN?
8. What are Samurai Bonds?

Chapter 9

International Taxation

9.1 INTRODUCTION

International Taxation assumes significance since the same income can be taxed twice in two countries, one in the country of accrual and the other in the country of residence of person or entity which receives the income.

Section 91 of the IT act talks about giving unilateral relief for foreign taxes paid against Indian taxes. India has entered into Double Taxation Avoidance Agreement with many countries. Since DTAA represents international agreement, the provisions as per the Indian Income Tax Act or international treaty whichever is favourable will be applied

In the case of Japan, it gives a provision of tax sparred margin to boost Japanese investment in India. For example if interest or dividend from investment in India is taxable at 10% but exempted through an exemption notification, then the tax credit will be given in Japan as if 10% tax has been levied, ignoring the exemption notification.

There are tax havens like Mauritius with which government of India has entered into DTAA by which income accruing to entities in Mauritius are taxed at special rates or exempted. Due to this investments are routed by companies in other countries by forming entities in Mauritius and routing the investment through them. This is called as *Mauritius route*.

Similarly, leasing agreements are done in such a manner that the transaction is known as *leasing* in one country and *hire purchase* in the other country leading to claiming of double depreciation and consequently two tax benefits in two different countries known as *double dip*. Sometimes three depreciations are claimed for same transaction in three countries for tax purpose, this is called as *triple dip*.

But now due to the active stand taken by US Government tax havens, tax sparred margins, and double and triple dip depreciations are becoming increasingly rare.

MNCs employ *transfer pricing* as a tax saving device for transaction between two branches or subsidiaries. In addition to this, they use royalties and fees for technical services to skim profits from high taxation countries to tax havens. This process has been accentuated by the lowering of tariff as well as liberalization of exchange controls. In recognition of the same, authorities in developing countries are incorporating transfer pricing regulations in their tax laws.

9.2 ACCOUNTING FOREIGN EXCHANGE

In the case of regular transaction like trading in goods and services foreign exchange is booked on the date of transaction and its value is restated at the exchange rate prevailing on the date of preparing profit and loss account and balance sheet. In the case of items for which forward covers are booked, the proportionate premium from the date of transaction and the date of financial statement is used to restate asset and liability and the difference is charged to profit and loss account.

For foreign branches and subsidiaries, all current assets and liabilities are restated at the exchange rate on which financial statements are prepared while non-current assets are stated at historical exchange rate with depreciation being accounted at the same exchange rate at which the assets are accounted.

Instead of current assets and liability classification, assets and liabilities are classified as monetary assets and liabilities and non-monetary assets and liabilities. While monetary assets and liabilities are restated at closing rate, non-monetary assets and liabilities are stated at the rate prevailing on the date of transaction. The main difference between the method as given above is that inventory being non-monetary asset is stated at historical cost even though it is a current asset.

In a single exchange rate system all change in exchange rate is treated as part of cost of goods.

In two exchange rate transactions, change in the exchange rate between the dates of transaction to closing of books are treated either as a gain or loss to be accounted in the accounting period or deferred and adjusted at the time of settlement of transaction and not charged to the goods.

Revenue and expenditure other than depreciation are translated at the average rate or the rate prevailing on the date of transaction, depreciation is translated at the same rate at which the underlying assets are translated.

In India, Accounting Standard 11 AS11 issued by the Institute of Chartered Accountants of India is applicable for Foreign Exchange Accounting.

Difference between Indian and International Accounting Standards and US GAAP:

S. No.	Indian Standard	US GAAP
1.	Has to be prepared Schedule VI of Companies Act	No such requirement as long as it complies with US GAAP
2.	Preliminary expense treated as assets and written off on deferred basis	No concept as preliminary expenses
3.	Completed contract method accepted	Completed contract method not accepted
4.	Research & Development cost can be capitalized on certain specified criteria	R&D expenditure to be expensed
5.	Accrued losses from firm Commitment not recognized in financial statements	They are recognized in financial statements
6.	Accounting standards exist for accounting Government grants	No such accounting standard exists
7.	No need to disclose current portion of long term loan separately	Current portion of long term loan to be disclosed separately

S. No.	Indian Standard	US GAAP
8.	Combination method recognized for amalgamation	Combination method dose not exist for amalgamation
9.	Consolidation method for holding accounts optional	Consolidation method is compulsory

It should be recognized that there were many more variants between Indian and US GAAP but due to the efforts of SEBI and Institute of Chartered Accountants of India, many of these gaps have been bridged to ensure transparency in reporting and corporate governance.

At the time of Entering into Transaction of purchase involving 1,00,000 Euros Exchange rate between Rupee/Euro was 50/Euro. On the balance sheet date exchange rate was 52/Euro. Date of settlement exchange rate is 53/ Euro. Draw Journal entries under single transaction or two transaction system.

Single Transaction

At the time of entering into transaction.

Purchase	Dr 50,00,000
Creditor	Cr 50,00,000

On the date of Balance Sheet

Purchase	Dr 2,00,000
Creditor	Cr 2,00,000

On the date of Transaction

Creditor	Dr 52,00,000
Purchase	Dr 1,00,000
Payment	Cr 53,00,000

Two Transaction system

At the time of transaction

Purchase	Dr 50,00,000
Creditor	Cr 50,00,000
Loss on Exchange	Dr 2,00,000
Creditor	Cr 2,00,000

At the time of settlement

Creditor	Dr	52,00,000
Loss on exchange	Dr	1,00,000
Payment	Cr	53,00,000.

9.3 APPRAISAL OF INTERNATIONAL CAPITAL PROJECT

International project involves country risk, which further involves political risk in the form of adverse policies being pursued against international capital, discriminatory taxation, and restriction on repatriation. In addition to this, change in exchange rates as well as transfer pricing problem and loss of existing export income are risks involved in evaluating foreign project.

To get over the country risk, the firm finances its foreign investment in the form of debt, since it is easy to repatriate debt capital as well as interest in the event of adverse changes in Balance of Payment position, than for equity capital and dividend. Similarly, leasing of equipment acts as an effective antidote against country risk due to the facility given for seizing the equipment in the event of non-payment, as well as lease rental being more in the nature of interest on loan is allowed for free repatriation even in the case of restriction on repatriation of dividends. In borrowing as well as in financial leasing which is akin to borrowing exchange risk is borne by borrower and not the investor. Apart from this, both interest on borrowing and lease charges being in the nature of charge on profit will be paid irrespective of the fact whether profit is there or not, as in the case of dividends. Interest on borrowing as well as lease charges are definite unlike dividends which are discretionary.

International projects are evaluated based on Adjusted Present Value method (APV) instead of Net Present Value (NPV) as in the case of normal evaluation of capital project. This involves unbundling of risk and applying different discount rates for different cash flows like tax benefit on depreciation, tax benefit on additional borrowing capacity, concessional loans provided by the host country, tax benefit of transfer pricing, Exchange risk on regular cash flows as well as activating fund from blocked accounts is also taken into consideration.

Thus, for increased borrowing capacity the tax benefit on the interest will be discounted at the risk free interest rate.

Tax benefit on depreciation will be discounted at the risk free interest rate, if the benefit of tax on depreciation is certain.

Since future cash flow is uncertain, it will be discounted at the all equity rates. Amount invested from blocked account will be reduced from the investment.

Concessional rate of interest given by host country will be discounted at normal rate of borrowing to arrive at the present value.

9.4 EXAMPLES

National Motors, an American automobile manufacturer is considering building a new plant in Britain to produce its sports car, Ferrari. The estimated construction cost of the plant is 50 million pounds, and the construction should be completed in a year. The plant will raise borrowing capacity to about 40 million dollars.

National Motors can reinvest 20 Million pounds already held in Britain. If these funds were repatriated to the US, they would face an effective tax rate of 46%. Inflation in Britain is expected to be at a 15% rate, while that in the US is put at 10% on an annual basis.

The current exchange rate is $/ Pound sterling = 2, and the purchasing power parity is likely to hold.

National Motors hopes to maintain its technological lead in Britain only for five years. The firm expects to sell 10,000 cars per year. The initial sticker price is 8000 pounds with current production costs works out at 6000 pounds per car.

Because National Motors will be building the new plant in Merseyside, an area of heavy unemployment, the British Government has offered the company a loan of 20 million pounds at 10% interest rate. The loan is to be repaid in five equal annual installments.

The competitive rate is 20% while in the United States, National Motors can borrow at 12%.

The tax rate in Britain is 40% (with permissible depreciation of car over five years). The British and US tax authorities are careful that appropriate transfer prices are used so that no taxes are saved on that account. National Motors believes that a 20% return is appropriate for the purpose of capital budgeting.

Calculate adjusted present value.

Exchange rates for six years

1st Year	=	2(1.10)/ (1.15) = 1.91
2nd Year	=	1.83
3rd Year	=	1.75
4th Year	=	1.67
5th Year	=	1.60
6th Year	=	1.53

Since the investment goes till end of first year average exchange rate of pound sterling = 1.95$ can be taken for initial investment.

If 20 million pound in UK is repatriated tax in US is 9.2 million pound. Thus by not repatriating and investing the funds in UK this amount can be saved thus the initial investment can be taken as (50–9.2) = 40.8 million pound.

Converted at 1.95$ initial investment in terms of dollar is = 79.56 million $.

Cash flow for each year is 2000 pound sterling into 10,000 cars = 2,00, 000,00 pounds.

Tax rate as per UK or US whichever is high to be taken, so applicable tax rate is 46%.

Post tax cash flow is = 1,08,00,000 pounds.

Can be discounted at 20% for five years = 1,08.00.000 * 1.83/1.20+ 1,08,00,000 * 1.75/(1.20)^2+ 1,08,00,000 * 1.67/(1.20)^3 + 1,08,00,000 * 1.60/(1.20) ^ 4+ 1,08,00,000 * 1.53/(1.20) ^ 5.

= 16470000$+ 13125000$ + 10425433$+ 8347826$+6662903$

= 55031162$

Return on investment is highly risky thus it is discounted at all equity rates.

Tax benefit on depreciation

Depreciation = 5000000/5= 10,00,0000 pounds (assuming salvage value to be nil)

Assuming risk free interest rate to be 10% being equivalent of US inflation rate and tax rate as 46% being higher of US and British rates tax benefit on depreciation for five years

= 10000000*.46*1.83/1.10 + 10000000 * .46 * 1.75/(1.10) ^ 2 + 10000000 * .46 * 1.67/(1.10) ^ 3 + 10000000 * .46 * 1.60/(1.10) ^ 4 + 10000000 * .46 * 1.53/(1.10) ^ 5

= 7652727$+6652892$+ 5775940$+5041100$+ 4371435$

= 29494094$

Tax benefit on additional Borrowing capacity of 40 million dollars at 12%

= 4,00,00,000 * .12 * .46/(1.1) + 2208000/(1.1) ^ 2+ 2208000/(1.1) ^ 3 + 2208000/(1.1) ^ 4 + 2208000/(1.1) ^ 5

= 2007273+ 1824793+ 1660150+1512329+ 1371428

= 8375973$

Discounting is done at risk free rate.

Value of Concessional rate

Five installments =

1st Installment = 6 million pound

2nd installment = 5.6 million

3rd installment = 5.2 million

4th installment = 4.8 million

5th installment = 4.4 million

present value of concession = 6/(1.2)+ 5.6/(1.2) ^ 2 + 5.2/(1.2) ^ 3 + 4.8/(1.2) ^ 4 + 4.4/(1.2) ^4

= 5 + 3.89 + 3+ 2.31+ 1.77

= 20-15.97

= 4.03 million pounds

= 4.03* 1.91 $= 7.70 million $

There are no transfer pricing benefits.

Thus the APV is =100.59 million $.

Since the NPV is positive the project can be undertaken.

9.5 FINANCIAL MANAGEMENT IN MNCs

Multinationals have branches throughout the world. In some branches there are payables in particular currencies and in other branches there are receivables and by doing centralized management, netting can be done to effectively manage risk, which is not possible if decentralized management is practiced.

Similarly if centralized management is practiced the shortages in some centers can be ironed out with surplus in other centers as well as investment decisions of net short-term surplus can be taken with the best interest of the organization in mind. But while considering the short term surplus management factors like transaction cost, taxes and convenience should be taken into consideration. Thus, if the subsidiary is in London while the parent is in Sweden, if centralized cash management is practiced by the parent then the benefit of London being one of the best financial center is lost.

CONCLUSION

In this chapter we studied about evaluation of foreign projects based on APV method instead of NPV method, which involves unbundling various risks and applying appropriate discount rate depending on risk involved. Also we studied in detail the following topics: International taxation, concept of DTAA, Permanent Establishment, Tax Haven, international leasing as a tax planning mechanism, tax sparred margins, Accounting for foreign exchange relevant accounting standard involved, difference between US GAAP and Indian GAAP, advantages and disadvantages of centralized and decentralized cash management in a MNC.

SUGGESTED ASSIGNMENTS

1. Examine the difficulties involved in International Project appraisal.
2. What is meant by Country Risk?
3. Explain with suitable example how international lease transaction enables multinational firms to reduce taxes and political risk?
4. What are the important advantages of investing in foreign affiliates in the form of debt instead of equity?

Chapter 10

CASE STUDIES

10.1 CASE STUDY I

X Ltd., an Indian company opened LC for 6 Million Swedish Kroner for Import of two numbers of pulsed rectifier. It opened an Irrevocable LC in favour of Y Ltd., for 6 million Swedish Kroner. Swedish company shipped only one number pulsed rectifier but invoiced for 2 numbers of pulsed rectifiers. The Bill of lading says that the packing contains two numbers of pulsed rectifiers, Invoice and packing list also mentions about two numbers pulsed rectifier. State Bank of India, the banker for Indian company remitted the amount and debited the value to Indian company's accounts. Indian company wants to hold the banker responsible for short shipment, will it succeed?

Solution

Indian company will not succeed, since the foreign LC is subject to Uniform Customs and Practice for Documentary Credit (UCPDC 500). According to which LC is not payment against goods but only payment against documents. As far as the Banker is concerned, the documents as called for in the LC have been presented by the seller and there is no internecine discrepancy among the documents. Because of this he will not be held liable for short shipment of the goods, physically.

10.2 CASE STUDY II

A Japanese exporter has exported steel to an Indian Importer. One of the documents called for in the LC is Mills Testing Certificate in English language only. Mills certificate was printed in front side in English and back side in Japanese. Since the condition was in English language, the bank referred it to the Indian importer for waiver of discrepancy. Since, in the meantime the steel price fell deeply in International market, Indian Importer refused to waive the discrepancy and asked for reduction in price from Japanese exporter as a precondition for waiver of discrepancy. The Japanese Exporter wants to sue LC opening bank for withholding payment for such minor discrepancy, will he succeed?

International LC is subject to UCPDC 500 which clearly states that it is a payment against document and not payment against goods as far as the bank is concerned. Thus, the bank will be held responsible for making remittance even if there is some minor discrepancy against document. So, the Japanese exporter will not succeed.

10.3 CASE STUDY III

An Indian importer is planning to import. He asks you that by invoicing in which currency to minimize the exchange fluctuation.

In India $ is used as intervention currency. All other currencies exchange rates are determined by crossing rupee dollar rate with $ other currency rate as prevailing in International market. Thus, the standard deviation which determines the fluctuation of any currency for any currency against rupee is the multiple of standard deviation of rupee against dollar and dollar against the other currency and will be definitely higher than standard deviation of rupee against dollar. If Japanese exporter agrees Indian importer can ask him to bill in US$ to minimize exchange fluctuation.

10.4 CASE STUDY IV

An Indian importer importing green houses from US is given a 180 days credit by US exporter at US prime rates. He approaches you as a foreign exchange consultant to ascertain how to evaluate the credit. Whether interest has to be inbuilt into the price or to be charged separately, what factors are relevant?

Forward premium for one month with US prime rate for 180 days should be compared with Indian borrowing rate to ascertain whether to borrow in Foreign market or not.

For example if prime rate in US is 6% p.a. while 6 months forward premium is 4%, domestic rate is 12% p.a., better to borrow in domestic market since six months cost will be 6% instead of 7%, if exchange fluctuation is also taken into consideration.

If price is inbuilt then customs duty to be paid on interest is to be taken into consideration and this should be compared with withholding tax on interest to determine whether to build interest into price or to charge it separately.

10.5 CASE STUDY V

Prita owns a Garment unit. She got an export order from Departmental Store in US for 3,00,000 US $. During a party she meets you and discusses with you regarding export financing. You mention to her about packing credit facilities and she asks you to send her a brief note regarding the same. Draft a suitable note?

Note: Packing credits are extended to exporter based on export order or irrevocable LCs. Running packing credit facilities are extended for regular exporters without insisting on order copy at the time of exports. Packing credits are extended to exporters as and when required.

There is pre-shipment packing credit and post-shipment packing credit. They are extended for a maximum period of 180 days with a further provision of extension by 90 days at the discretion of bank. Pre-shipment credits are extended for procuring material, manufacturing, storing finished goods, post-shipment credits are extended against export receivables.

Packing credit is given in the form of rupee packing credit as well as packing credit in foreign currency.

Rupee packing credits are extended at Prime Lending Rates of the Bank – 2.5%, while Foreign Currency packing credits are extended at any one of the four currencies (US$, Pound Sterling, Japanese Yen, Euro at Libor + .75%).

Sometimes Rupee packing credit will have negative interest rates. For example Prime rate is 12%, so the rupee packing credit will be 9.5% per annum, 180 days rate will be 4.75%, if the invoicing is done in dollar and credit period is 180 days and dollar quotes at a premium of 6% for 6 months against rupee, the real interest rate is - 1.25%.

ECGC cover is must for packing credit and the same can be liquidated only out of export proceeds. Margins will be at the discretion of bank.

10.6 CASE STUDY VI

Mr. Gupta is planning to set up a factory with foreign collaboration for manufacture of footwear, while greater part of the turnover will be exported to foreign parent under buyback agreement, he also wants to cater to the needs of domestic market, he meets you- an Import Export consultant–in a marriage function and asks you about the various benefits given by Government of India for exporters. Prepare a note explaining various benefits available to exporters.

Pre Export Benefits

1. Advance license for duty free import of material for use in export.
2. Export Promotion Capital Goods (EPCG) scheme for import of capital goods against undertaking export obligation based on customs duty saved, whereby duty can be paid at 5% instead of normal rates).

Post Export Benefits

1. Duty Free Replenishment Certificate (DFRC) for items for which Standard Input Output Norm (SION) is available for import of items used for exports subject to minimum value addition of 25%. It can be obtained after export and realization of export proceeds. It can be used by the exporter himself for import of material or transferred for a premium.
2. Duty Entitlement Pass Book Scheme (DEPB) under which duty credit is given, based on exports for item for which SION is available. This is given after export of items and realization of sale proceeds. This can be used for importing any item, but some restrictions are there for import of sensitive items, Customs also have the right to verify export value to prevent over valuation for

claiming excessive benefits. Either the exporter himself can use it or sell it for a premium.

3. Duty Drawback can be availed by exporter who has paid customs duty on imported material, as well as excise duty on indigenous material on which Cenvat benefit is not claimed, which is used for export production.

4. If 50% or more of production is exported the unit can be set up as Export Oriented Unit (EOU) in any one of the 300 places notified as customs warehousing station by Central Board of Excise and Customs (CBEC), can work under Customs Bond. EOUs are not allowed to do trading. EOUs can import raw material, components, and capital goods without payment of customs duty and procure local materials as well as capital goods without payment of excise duty. EOUs can sell 50% of their production in domestic market by paying excise duty equivalent to 50% customs duty, if the item is imported. If imported raw material, components and consumables are used in manufacture of product or excise duty whichever is higher, otherwise if the products are manufactured out of wholly indigenous inputs 30% of customs duty or excise duty whichever is higher can be paid as excise duty.

5. If the unit does not want to work under Customs Bonding, it can be set up as Special Economic Zones (SEZ) at specified places. They can procure imported raw material, component and capital goods, without paying customs duty, indigenous raw material, components, and capital goods without paying excise duty.

6. Supplies made to EOU/ SEZ are exempted from excise duty and they are given benefits like Duty Drawback, DFRC, Advance license thereby treating the same as deemed exports by the Ministry of Commerce.

Apart from this, many State Governments exempt sales tax on material used for exports, as well as material and capital goods supplied to EOUs/ SEZ. Development Commissioner will refund Central sales tax paid for raw material, components, and capital goods etc.

Apart from this, income tax benefit is available for 90% of export profits.

10.7 CASE STUDY VII

Reema owns a company. Regular imports were made by the company. There was nearly a million dollar liability maturing over a period of 6 months. There was no exchange risk management in the company. Recently during a conversation with a banker terms like Hedging and derivatives were used. She would like to know how to use derivatives for managing her exchange risk from you as a Foreign Exchange Consultant.

Forwards, futures, options and swaps are derivatives used to hedge in exchange rate risk. The organization should decide a policy of active hedging or passive hedging or no hedging which is highly risky and speculative. In passive hedging all future payments will be hedged through derivatives like forward. In active hedging the organization constantly studies the exchange rate movement and decides on the extent of hedging and the type of instrument to be used for hedging.

For example, if the client feels that the rupee will depreciate much more than the forward rates, presently being quoted against dollar, then he can lock in his liability in the form of Forward cover, if he is sure about large variation in exchange rate but is not sure about the direction of exchange rate movement he can go for cross currency option or rupee option introduced recently. An upfront premium has to be paid for options.

The policy on hedging has to be determined by the governing body of the company. Use of derivatives for speculative purpose is anyhow not permitted in India. Suitable MIS to be installed to ascertain whether the policy laid down has been followed or not.

10.8 CASE STUDY VIII

Mr. Sharma, a businessman owning a medium scale garment unit is planning to borrow 5 million $ at Libor + 1.25%, three months from now for a period of five years and Libor is 6 months. Libor is to be reset every six months. He expects interest rates to go up, he asks advice from you as a treasurer in Foreign bank to protect himself from adverse interest rate change.

He can protect himself through an Interest Rate Swap (IRS) whereby he can pay fixed interest rate and receive floating interest rate, or through Forward rate agreement purchase whereby for the notional deposit of 5 million $ to be made three months from now he can get any excess of interest rate over the capped rate and should pay the difference in interest rate if the interest rate falls below the capped rate.

He can also go for interest rate cap purchase and being an option should pay an upfront premium.

Which one of the derivative to choose depends on the certainty, with which he expects the interest rate to rise, and the option premium...?

10.9 CASE STUDY IX

A Unit engaged in Bio. Technology exports flower shoots to Holland. The item is airlifted since it is perishable in nature. As per the terms of trade only if the offshoots are planted and if it yields desired flowers it will be paid for. Usually 5% to 10% fail during such plantation and will remain unpaid. Most of the consignments are small in value. In view of the smallness in value as well as high bank charges, especially, foreign bank charges, the unit wants to directly send the documents to the supplier. Suggest the points to be highlighted in its request to authorized dealer for permission for direct negotiation as well as the safeguard to be adopted by the unit for proper payment.

1. Since the product is perishable in nature, it is airlifted and directly delivered to the supplier. Under such circumstances routing of the document through bank is only symbolic and does not serve any purpose, but it is costly in the form of high foreign bank charges.
2. Even though direct negotiation is allowed for SEZ and status holders, RBI through its circular clearly authorizes the authorized dealer to exercise its discretion and give permission in any other cases. In view of the above mentioned reasons, this is considered as a fit case.
3. In view of the perishable nature of the consignment, it is generally permitted to load 5 to 10% more than the invoiced quantity to get over the problem of unproductive off shoots.
4. ECGC to be informed, suitable credit limit to be fixed for each importer in Holland after proper credit appraisal to avoid default.

10.10 CASE STUDY X

Mr. X deals in press tools and he has received a first time export order of 1,00,000 $ from a department stores in US$, he asks you for the information on various documentation formalities for exports, as export import consultant.

If the export is against LC, it should be ensured that the documents called for in the LC should be meticulously prepared to get payment, since LC is payment against document and not payment against goods and any slight discrepancy will lead to stoppage of payment.

If the export is by way of open credit, suitable credit enquiries to be made and ECGC cover to be taken.

Normal documents involved in exports are:

1. Invoice.
2. Packing list.
3. Shipping Bill (There are various shipping bills like Drawback shipping bill, DEPB Shipping bill, DFRC shipping bill and declaration regarding Drawback and advance license should accompany shipping bill)
4. GR Forms, SDF, PP for export of goods either through manual customs mode or EDI Customs mode or through post to be prepared in duplicate.
5. Softex formats are prepared for software exports.
6. GR/SDF Form will be certified by Customs for value, PP form for postal exports will be certified by authorized dealers, Softex form will be certified by STPI.
7. GSP (Generalized System of Preference) duly certified by Export promotion council wherever concessional duty is applicable.
8. Invoice, packing list, Exchange control copy of shipping bill, Exchange control copy of GR form should be negotiated through bank within 21 days from the date of BL.
9. Bank realization certificate should be taken from the collecting Bank for realization of export proceeds.
10. Legal Undertaking should be executed with Excise authorities and ARE 1 form to be prepared in quintuplicate, since exports are exempted from Excise.

11. If Amount is received in advance Foreign Inward Remittance Certificate to be obtained.
12. Policy covering Credit and political risk to be taken from Export Credit Guarantee Corporation.
13. Product liability insurance can be taken.

10.11 CASE STUDY XI

There is a huge opportunity for exporting Machine Tools to Tanzania. But the Tariff structure of Tanzania acts as an impediment. X Co Ltd., a Machine tool manufacturer asks for your advice.

1. X Company Ltd., can plan Foreign Direct Investment in Tanzania instead of India to overcome the Tariff Barrier.
2. But Foreign Direct Investment is risky in the form of political risks like restriction on repatriation of profits, nationalization and expropriation.
3. Apart from this there is also exchange rate risk.
4. These factors should be taken into consideration while evaluating discount rates for cash flow.
5. As an antidote to risk a minimum discounted payback period of 3 years can be fixed as acceptance criteria for the project.

10.12 CASE STUDY XII

X Co Ltd., is planning to Finance a Foreign Project. He approaches you for means of Financing. Explain the various sources available as well as the advantage, disadvantage associated with the same.

1. Syndicated Loans: Syndicated Loans can be availed from Banks. Advantage is they are wholesale in nature due to which the credit terms can be easily renegotiated. Exchange risk can be managed through taking loan with multicurrency option.
2. Euro Bonds: Euro Bonds are medium term instrument. They are bearer in nature, with very little disclosure and regulatory requirements like registration, compulsory credit rating, they are cheaper than foreign bonds.

3. Foreign Bonds: Foreign Bonds have many regulatory requirements like withholding tax, credit rating, registration. But they can be taken for much larger period.
4. In debt instrument exchange risk to be borne by borrower.

Equity instruments like GDR, ADR to be used. In GDR and ADR exchange risk is borne by the investor, they have no repayment period. But disclosure requirements are much higher especially in ADR market where the issuer has to restate his accounts as per US GAAP, register with SEC and comply with SEC disclosure requirements. In spite of this the market is popular due to it's depth and the prestige it offers.

Chapter 11

Solved Model Papers

11.1 MODEL PAPER I

What do you understand by Foreign Exchange Market?

When an exporter or importer is exporting or importing at least one party has to deal in Foreign Currency. Due to this, there exists a market for foreign exchange. This exists through an informal market like Bankers, brokers, importers, exporters called as OTC market. It is also done through organized market and it is called as exchange traded market. These exchanges are in various places throughout the world like New York, London, Frankfurt, Tokyo, Bahrain, Singapore, Zurich, Hong Kong, Sydney and it is a 24 hour market.

Name Major players in Foreign Exchange Markets. Briefly write what their roles are.

The Major players in Foreign Exchange Markets are:

- Commercial Banks
- Central Banks
- Brokers
- Large Corporates
- Hedge Funds.

Commercial Banks: Commercial Banks buy and sell Foreign exchange, give two way quotes and act as market makers, the market in which Commercial Banks deal with Individuals and corporates are called as

Retail Market while inter-bank Market is called as wholesale market. The volumes in the Wholesale market are much more than the volumes in retail market.

Central Banks: Central Banks mainly operate to iron out fluctuation in the Foreign Exchange Market. In countries where exchange control operates Central Bank will regulate Foreign Exchange Market.

Brokers: Brokers as such do not deal in foreign exchange. They bring the buyer and seller together and charge a commission. They help in keeping the identity of person dealing in Foreign exchange secret, and also keep the direction of the deal secret till the quotes are obtained. They specialize in one or two currencies and keep themselves up to date about all aspects of the currency.

Large Corporates : Large corporates who have required expertise on their own deal in Foreign exchange market not only to hedge their risks, but also to speculate in currencies, and treat foreign exchange dealings as part of their treasury operations and as profit centre.

Hedge Funds: They obtain funds through high net worth individuals and not through market thereby keep themselves away from market scrutiny. They move their resources throughout the world in search of short term returns. The advent of information technology has facilitated this process. This money movement is also popularly called as hot money.

Discuss in detail with examples, the rules governing settlement date for spot and forward transaction?

Settlement date for spot transaction is two business days after the transaction is concluded. That means the two business days between the date of transaction and date of settlement should not be a holiday in settlement location or dealing location. For example an Indian and German Bank exchange US $ for Pound Sterling then the settlement locations are US and UK and dealing locations are India and Germany. If the two Business days after the settlement turns out to be a holiday in one of the locations US, UK, India, Germany then the value date will shift to next business day in all the locations. For example transaction entered on 25th October will be settled on 27th October if it is not a holiday in any one of the locations.

In the case of Forward contract first the spot value date is determined and whole month and not 30 or 31 days is added to arrive at the value date. For example if a Forward contract is entered on 25th October value date for spot is 27th October and one month will be added if it is for first month delivery and value date will be 27th

November provided it is not a holiday in any of the centers. If it is a holiday in any one of the centers value date will be next business day in all the locations.

But if the value date of a forward contract falls on the last day of the month and that turns out to be a holiday then the previous business day and not the subsequent business day which falls on next month will be treated as value date.

11.2 MODEL PAPER II

Why are Balance of Payment statistics important?

Exchange rates are determined by many factors. One of the important factors is demand and supply. In a truly floating rate regime, higher the demand the currency will appreciate and lower the demand the currency will depreciate. Balance of payment statistics indicate whether the demand for the currency is increasing (Balance of Payment being positive) or on decline (Balance of Payment being negative). Even in a fixed exchange rate regime corrections are made in exchange rates to correct chronic problems in Balance of Payment. Apart from these a country will raise interest rate to avoid devaluation by increasing interest rate. Thus, the Finance Manager can track future monetary policies and interest rates by keeping a close tab on Balance of Payment statistics. Similarly negative Balance of payment will lead to curb in Government spending and increase in taxes and surplus in Balance of Payment will lead to increase in Government spending and cut in taxes, these informations will be of great use to a Finance Manager.

Explain briefly the factors that affect exchange rate?

Purchasing Power Parity theory states that the difference in Exchange rate is due to difference in inflation rate between two currencies. Otherwise there is scope for arbitrage. Purchasing power parity ignores, transaction cost, taxes, transportation cost, tariff, and non-tariff barriers.

But in a market dominated by speculators if inflation is higher in a country in expectation of hike in short term interest rate in the country to counter inflation short term money or hot money moves in thereby the currency of a country having higher inflation appreciates instead of depreciating.

Interest rate parity theory suggests that the difference in exchange rate is difference in interest rate. Higher the interest rate, lower the exchange rate otherwise, arbitrage will take place. But interest rate parity does not recognize exchange control, transaction costs and taxes.

Forces of demand and supply determine the exchange rates as evidenced by BOP statistics.

Political Factors also determine the exchange rates.

Thus, it can be said that the interest rate, inflation, political factors, tariff, transaction cost, taxes, demand and supply determine the exchange rate.

On 15th September, you receive a mail transfer from your New York correspondent for US $ 5,000 payable to your customer. Your account with the correspondent Bank has been credited with the amount of mail transfer in reimbursement.

Assuming Rupee/ US Dollars are quoted in the local inter-bank market as

Spot USD = Rs 44.2500/2700

Spot October 2200/2320

Calculate the exchange rate and the rupee amount payable to the customer if an exchange margin of .080% is allowed.

Transit time can be taken as 21 days. October spot rate is 44.4700 / 44.5020. Swap points are in ascending order thereby suggesting it is premium.

October buying rate is 44.4700. Since it is purchase of dollar margin to be deducted

Thus the amount to be payable is = (44.4700 * .9992) = 44.43

Thus the rupee to be credited to customer is = 5000*44.43=222150 Rs.

11.3 MODEL PAPER III

What do you mean by full convertibility of Rupee?

Indian Rupee is not traded outside India. It is subjected to restriction under Foreign Exchange Management whereby conversion of Indian Rupee to Foreign currency is done through authorized persons who are authorized by Reserve Bank of India. FEMA classifies transaction into current account and Capital account transaction, while current account transactions are substantially liberalized under FEMA, Capital account is subject to restrictions.

Full convertibility means that the rupee can be freely converted into any foreign currency without going through authorized person.

Explain "Buy low and sell high, buy high and sell low" with an example for each.

In direct quote for rupee against dollar how many units of Rs per $ is given

For example $ = 46.50/47

That means the trader will buy one $ for 46.50 Rs and sell one $ for 47 Rs the difference .50 paise between the buying and selling rate is called selling buying spread or simply spread, which represents the profits of the dealer. Thus in direct quote the dealer makes profit by buying low and selling high.

Thus, buy low and sell high applies for the market, while buy high and sell low applies to a person who deals with the market.

You, as the forex dealer of your bank, are informed that the bank has sold a TT on Rome for Italian Lira 50,000,000 at the rate of 100 Lira = 2.44 Rs. You are required to cover Transaction through London or New York, whichever offers you better profits. The rates on that date are:

Mumbai-London : Rs. 46.75/ 46.80

Mumbai-New York : Rs. 31.30/31.35

London-Rome : Lira 1927.5/ 1930.5

New York- Rome : .076980 US cents/ .077580 US cents.

Will you cover the transaction through London or New York.? What will be the exchange profit on transaction? Ignore brokerage.

Through New York

Rs/ Lira = Rs/$ $/100lira= 31.30*.076980/31.35*.077580

= 2.4094 /2.4321

Through London

Rs/Lira = Rs/PS * PS/Lira

Lira/ PS = 1927.5/1930.5

PS/Lira = 1/1930.5/1/1927.5

= .000518/.000519

Rs/ Lira = 46.75* .000518/46.8* .000519

= .024217/.024289

Rs/ 100 Lira = 2.4217/2.4289

In New York market one has to pay 2.4321 Rs to get 100 Lira while in London 2.4289 Rs to be paid to get 100 Lira, thus it is cheaper to buy in London Market at 2.4289 Rs/ 100 Lira.

Purchase price of 100 Lira 2.4289 and sell at 2.44 for 100 lira there by making .0111 Rs for 100 lira for 500,000,000 Lira total profit is

= (500000000/100) .0111= Rs 55,500.

11.4 MODEL PAPER IV

Name six major risks in forex dealings?

- Market Risk
- Credit Risk
- Operations Risks
- Legal Risk
- Liquidity Risk
- Systemic Risk

What are the advantages of SWIFT?

Swift means Society for Worldwide Inter Bank Financial Telecommunication. The major beneficiaries are banks, brokers, corporates, investment managers, security exchanges, central depositories and clearing corporations.

Major benefits of SWIFT are replacement of paper based procedures through automated procedures using swift standards. Swift's markets are financial institutions conducting business in payments, foreign exchange, money market, security trading and trade finance.

Swift provides secure and reliable data communication, which are secure, reliable, competitively priced and are supported by 1200 organizations of professionals in financial services throughout the world.

Increasing productivity, cost reduction, control of financial risks, through end to end financial transaction processing between financial institution and their customers.

What is Future contract? Explain the salient features of Future contract?

Futures are exchange traded derivatives. Delivery period and quantity are standard in exchange traded derivatives like futures and only price is left to be determined by market. There is active secondary market for future. Clearing house of the exchange acts as counter party, thereby removing counter party risk. Thus future facilitates price discovery.

Clearing house protects itself in the form of margining like initial margin, maintenance margin and mark to market margin or variation margin.

Futures are used for hedging as well as speculative purpose.

In futures the underlying may be commodity, interest rate risk, foreign exchange or index or a security like share.

Futures being a standard contract will not act as perfect hedge.

Futures can be settled through delivery, squaring off or settlement of difference in cash.

11.5 MODEL PAPER V

What is Translation Exposure? Give an example.

Translation exposure arises due to the need to convert foreign currency denominated assets and liabilities. Thus a Company has foreign Branch. The statement of assets and liabilities will be incorporated into the Company's Balance Sheet by converting the same into domestic currency. Translation exposure is also called as accounting exposure.

What is Interest Rate Risk? Explain Interest Rate Risk with reference to Income Risk and Capital Risk?

If fixed interest securities are held subsequently if the interest rate rises the reinvestment income will rise while the value of the security will fall. The extent of increase in income is not equal to fall in value of securities.

The period for which the security should be held whereby the extent of increase in reinvestment income is equal to fall in price of security is called as duration which is a sophisticated interest rate risk management tool.

The fall in interest rate will also lead to the same effect in reverse direction. Thus it can be seen that the rise or fall in the interest rate will have opposite effect on capital value and reinvestment income.

Explain the theories:

1. ***PPP***
2. ***Interest Rate Parity***

PPP: Is known as purchasing power parity. It says that the change in the exchange rate in two currencies can be explained by the difference in inflation rate to avoid any arbitrage. Countries which have higher inflation will see their currencies depreciate; while those with lower inflation rate will see their currencies appreciate.

PPP has several defects; like that the basket of goods and services used for measuring inflation varies from country to country. PPP assumes that there are no transaction costs, transportation, taxes, tariff barrier which are unrealistic assumptions. PPP will be usually applicable if the market is dominated by Fundamental forces like Government or Central banks and not by speculators as of now.

There is very little empirical evidence in support of PPP.

Interest Rate Parity: As per interest rate parity the difference in exchange rate between two currencies is due to difference in interest rates. The currency with higher interest rate will suffer depreciation, while currency with lower interest rate will appreciate. If the difference in exchange rate is not difference in interest rate it will lead to opportunity for arbitrage. But interest rate parity theory does not assume transaction cost, exchange control and withholding taxes which makes the theory unrealistic.

11.6 MODEL PAPER VI

Can you fully hedge Forex risk? Explain.

There are three types of forex risks:

- Transaction exposure,
- Translation exposure and
- Economic exposure.

Transaction exposure can be fully hedged through Forwards and Options, Translation exposure can be hedged through swap, while economic exposure arises due to liberalization of economy which is influenced by competitor's action which cannot be fully hedged.

How can you cover Transaction exposure, Economic exposure? Give an example of each.

Transaction exposure are short term in nature like exposure due to short term receivables are payables, for example an importer has to pay 1,00,000 US$ after 90 days can cover the same using Forward cover or option fully depending on whether relatively how certain he feels about the extent or direction of the movement. He can use futures to hedge the exposure. But future being exchange traded instrument and standardized will not act as perfect hedge.

Economic exposure arises due to opening up of economy. Even though a firm may not have any Foreign exchange transaction, if the competitor imports his materials from Japan and pays the same in Japanese Yen, any appreciation of rupee against yen will make his cost structure cheaper; thereby he can pass on the same garner larger market share. The firm can tackle this by borrowing its fund requirements in yen. If yen depreciates it's interest and principal payment in terms of Indian rupee will decrease leading to lower cost structure which can be used to neutralize the competitor's action.

What is an LC? Mention the different types of LC.

LC is letter of credit. In trade if the seller and the buyer do not know each other then the seller wants payment before he sends the goods, while the buyer wants to receive the goods and examine the same before he makes payment. This may lead to stalemate. To avoid this the buyer's bank intervenes and assures seller that it will pay the seller if proper documents as called for in the LC are presented irrespective of the fact whether the buyer reimburses the same or not. Thus LC lubricates the wheels of commerce.

LC is a payment against documents and not payment against goods. Thus the Bank is not concerned about the nature and quality of physical goods, but only will see whether the proper documents as called for in the LC are presented before it makes the payments. As a corollary even if the Bank ignores slight discrepancy in the document the opener can refuse to pay.

The parties to LC are Opener, opening Bank, advising Bank, negotiating bank, beneficiary. International LCs are subject to UCPDC 500 which is evolved by International Chamber of Commerce.

The various types of LC are:

- Irrevocable LC
- Revocable LC
- Confirmed LC
- Transferable LC
- Back to back LC
- Red Clause LC
- Green Clause LC.

What is the difference between Bill of Lading and Bill of Exchange?

1. Bill of lading is a document of title, while bill of exchange is not a document of Title.
2. Bill of exchange requires acceptance, while bill of lading does not require any acceptance.
3. Bill of lading is a document evidencing receipt of the goods by the shipper, while bill of exchange is an evidence of acceptance of goods by drawee.

Write a note on:

1. **International Portfolio Management**
2. **Future Contact**
3. **Forward Rate Agreement.**

International Portfolio Management: As per the theory of Markowitz risk can be reduced by diversifying among negatively correlated cash flow.

Wealth maximization can be achieved by either reducing the risk for same level of return or increasing the return for same level of risk. In matured markets returns as well as risks are low. Emerging markets and matured markets are not perfectly positively correlated due to prevalence of artificial barrier like exchange control and information asymmetry. Thus an investor in matured market can increase his return without correspondingly increasing his risk leading to wealth maximization. From the point of view of emerging market due to portfolio investment secondary market liquidity will increase leading to increase in primary market activities leading to creation of wealth. Apart from this portfolio investment will lead to transfer of international best practices.

Future Contract: Future contracts are exchange traded, they are standard, due to which they have high level of liquidity, the clearing house of the exchange acts as the guarantor for these transactions, thereby no counter party risk is present facilitating price discovery. The underlying for a clearing contract is exchange rates, interest rates, security or an index. Futures due to their standardization do not act as perfect hedge. Clearing house protects it's position by initial margin and daily variation margin by marking to market.

Forward Rate Agreement: Forward rate agreements or FRAs are swap transactions which can be used to protect rise or fall in future interest rate. For example a corporate which is planning to raise loan in future can protect its position due to rise in interest rate by purchasing FRAs. In FRAs a notional deposit equivalent to the amount of FRA purchased is placed with the writer of FRAs. Any increase in interest over the contracted rate is paid by writer of FRA to the purchaser, but any fall in interest rate will be paid by purchaser to the writer. Vice versa procedure can be adopted for future investments to protect fall in interest rate.

Explain the role of World Bank.

World Bank or International Bank of Reconstruction and Development was established in 1944 in Bretton Wood and it is one of Bretton Wood twins.

Its main purpose was for aiding Economies ravaged by war and helping in their reconstruction and lending for development projects in developing countries. It lends at 1/2 % more than its average borrowing cost and interest rates are re-fixed every six months. Of late, World Bank has started giving loans for facilitating financial sector reforms and it acts as co-lender with commercial banks for financing projects where it finances the portion of the loan with longer maturity and allows commercial banks to take back its loan within a shorter maturity period. It also acts as a guarantor for loans by commercial Banks.

International Finance Corporation (IFC) is an arm of World Bank which finances private sector projects. This was established in the year 1956.

International Development Agency (IDA) was established in the year 1960 and it is the soft lending window of World Bank which lends at concessional rates for projects in developing countries.

Difference between depreciation and devaluation of a currency.

In floating rate exchange regime the exchange rate is determined by forces of demand and supply which leads to gradual decline in the exchange rate of a currency called as depreciation, while in fixed exchange rate one off adjustments are made in exchange rate called as devaluation.

What is offshore Banking? What are its advantages?

Offshore banking means having a branch or subsidiary in important financial centers instead of correspondent bank. Offshore banking enables to keep up to date on international financial information in spite of electronic systems giving up to date information like Reuters. It enhances the credit and investment decisions made through it's own employees. Apart from these many banks follow major customers in establishing offshore banks to provide services to its customers.

Apart from these if offshore banks are established commissions like negotiation, confirmation or advising can be made to accrue to bank's branch instead of correspondent bank. It also provides valuable opportunity for training its employees through it's offshore centers in multi-country and multi-cultural environment.

Offshore Branches and subsidiaries derisk the bank operations by spreading the country risk along several countries. It also allows the Bank to spread its customers throughout the world and removes concentration risk of doing excessive business with a single customer or a single region.

We should always borrow in a currency that is likely to devalue since it minimizes the cost of capital. Argue.

This is not always true. If the firm is going to import and export in a different currency if the borrowing is used to pay such imports due to such depreciation payment will become very costly. Similarly if the currency of exports is same as the currency of borrowing, any depreciation in currency which will reduce repayment cost but at the same time it will reduce export proceeds in terms of realization to offset the effect of depreciation.

If the currency of the borrowing is the currency of import, the depreciation of currency means inflation is increasing in that currency thereby increasing the price of the goods hence annulling any benefit due to depreciation in currency of borrowing.

If the currency depreciates interest rate will increase as per interest rate parity thereby annulling the benefit of depreciation in the form of higher interest rate unless the borrowing is done at floating rate.

If the borrowing is done at a fixed rate and there are no imports and exports then there will be benefit due to depreciation of the currency.

If derivatives are traded as part of treasury operations then instead of using money market we can use derivatives to get the same effect.

11.7 MODEL PAPER VII

Nature of Risk faced by Foreign exchange trader.

1. Market Risk
2. Credit Risk
3. Operations Risks
4. Legal Risk
5. Liquidity Risk
6. Systemic Risk.

Today Rupee is subject to Exchange Control under Foreign Exchange Management Act. An Indian cannot exchange Indian Rupee for Foreign Exchange straightaway but has to go through an authorized person who can be an authorized dealer or money changer.

FEMA has classified Foreign Exchange transactions into three categories like banned, restricted and free for current account purposes.

Current account is defined as those transactions which arise out of import or export of goods and services, travel, gifts and other normal dealings.

For example remittance for betting is a banned, current account transaction which is prohibited under FEMA.

There are many transactions which require permission from RBI, Central Government, like undertaking a foreign tour for cultural purpose which can be done only with the prior approval of Central Government.

There are free transactions like foreign travel for business purpose, remittance of gift to close relatives subject to certain limits which can be undertaken by authorized dealer without prior permission from RBI.

All transactions which do not fall within current account transaction category are called as capital account transaction such as: Issue of Foreign security, purchase of immovable property, exports of currency, Transfer of Foreign security, Holding Foreign currency bank account, giving guarantee to non-resident, borrowing from non-resident, lending to non resident by a resident are called as capital account.

Similarly, purchase of immovable property by non-resident in India, issue of security in India by non-resident, is also called as capital account transaction.

Even though current account transactions are liberalized, they are not yet made free.

Similarly, a capital account transaction which requires prior approval of RBI or Central Government is subject to clear cut guidelines.

Central Government as well as Reserve Bank wants to follow gradual liberalization of current and capital account transactions without embarking on full convertibility.

Compare and contrast comparative advantage theory with comparative cost theory.

1. Comparative advantage theory was propounded by David Ricardo, while Comparative Cost or Theory of Absolute Advantage was propounded by Adam Smith.
2. Both consider only labour cost.
3. In absolute advantage theory a nation can produce those articles where its cost of labour is cheaper compared to other nation and trade for Articles where other countries have absolute advantage thereby increase its as well as international wealth.

4. In Comparative Advantage, even if a nation enjoys absolute advantage it can manufacture those items where it has comparative advantage and can trade in other items to increase its as well as international wealth.
5. Principle for derivative swap is based on comparative advantage theory.
6. Both theories assume perfect competition as well as perfect mobility of labour which are not practical.
7. In both the theories only labour productivity is considered and increase in productivity due to technological innovations are ignored.
8. Both theories ignore transaction costs including transportation cost.
9. Both theories assume full employment of labour.
10. While absolute advantage theory explains the cause comparative advantage theory does not explain the cause.

What do you mean by Spot Rate and Forward Rate?

Spot rate means that rate in which delivery should be concluded within two business days from the date of transaction provided the concluding date is not a holiday in any of the centers of the transaction. If it is a holiday in any one of the transaction centers then next business day will be the date of conclusion of the transaction.

What are the important sources and causes for International Financial Flow?

Important sources are:

- Government Credit
- World Bank Finance
- IMF
- Syndicated Loans
- Money Market
- Euro Bond Market
- Foreign Bond Market
- Foreign Equity Market through Depositary Receipt
- Foreign Direct Investment
- Portfolio Management
- Hot Money.

Causes are:

1. Government Credit: It is given on bilateral basis either for development or for procuring arms.
2. World Bank Finance: World Bank finance is given for development programmes/projects.
3. IMF: IMF credits are given for tiding over exchange crisis.
4. Syndicated Loans: Syndicated loans are where huge credits are arranged by group of Banks through intermediation.
5. Money Market: Money markets are used for parking short term surpluses and for short term requirements.
6. Euro Bond Markets: Euro Bond Markets are medium term in nature and are used by borrowers who want very little regulations like credit rating and regulations.
7. Foreign Bond Markets: Foreign Bond Markets are used for long term needs.
8. Foreign Direct Investment: FDIs are made for diversifying unsystematic risk, to get over adverse exchange rate, tariff barriers etc.
9. Portfolio Management: Portfolio management is undertaken to mainly diversify unsystematic risk.
10. Hot Money: Hot money is short term money moving in search of quick returns. These are facilitated by technological revolution and e-banking.

Explain the concept of disequilibrium in Balance of Payment. How does disequilibrium arise? How it can be restored?

Balance of payment disequilibrium comes out of current account transaction, which involves exports of goods and services, transfer payments. Since they take place on their own to facilitate international trade they are called as autonomous transactions. If payment exceeds receipt it will lead to negative balance of payment where the country is said to be living beyond it's means. If receipt exceeds payment then balance of payment is positive and country is said to be living below it's means. In accountant's terminology they are called as above the line transactions.

This disequilibrium is financed through accommodating transactions like borrowing or lending in foreign exchange and they are called as above the line transactions.

Balance of payment disequilibrium can be understood by way of an equation.

$Y = C+G+I+X-M.$

Where

C = Consumption

G= Government expenditure

I = Investment

X = Export

M = Import

So Balance of payment is represented by equation

$X-M = Y-C-G-I$

$Y = C+T+S$

Where T is Taxes, S is savings

Substituting

$X-M = C+T+S-C-G-I$

$= (T-G) + S-I$

This clearly shows that Balance of payment disequilibrium, say, negative can be corrected by increasing taxes, decreasing Government expenditure, Increasing savings or reducing investment.

But all this will trigger recession and unemployment which the economy of developing country can ill bear. So borrowing for investing to correct the deficit is recommended.

Balance of payment deficit can also be corrected by increasing interest rate, depreciating exchange rate and making the investment climate in the country attractive for foreign capital.

What are the unique elements of international Financial System?

It is a 24 hour market with exchanges in New York, Frankfurt, London, Sydney, Bahrain, Singapore, and Tokyo operating round the clock. It has become very deep and wide and it can be cited as example of perfect capital market. It has bewildering varieties of instruments, with derivatives dominating the market. Due to information technology money gets transferred at lightning speed across the globe. This has made this a haven for speculators who move hot money across the globe in search of quick returns.

What is Depository Receipt? Explain with example ADR mechanism.

Depository receipts are innovation which was made by Morgan and Stanley to get over the regulations of US Pension Funds from investing in foreign securities. They are equity instruments. They are traded in OTC market as well as listed in exchange and traded. They are bearer instruments. They are two way fungible that is a deposit receipt can be converted to underlying shares and vice versa. Depository receipts can be classified as GDR, ADR and IDR (Global Depository Receipt, American Depository Receipt, and International Depository Receipt).

Suppose Infosys wants to issue 100 million $ ADR, the requirements are that first a depository Bank usually a Foreign Bank (say Citibank or Chase Manhattan Bank) is appointed. Shares are issued in the name of the depository Bank by Infosys. Physical custody of shares is held by a custodian bank which is usually an Indian Bank say ICICI Bank. The Depository Bank issues receipt that it is holding the shares and these receipts are listed and traded in New York, American Stock Exchange as well as NASDAQ.

These can be placed on private placement basis under rule 144A of the SEC regulations where it need not comply with SEC disclosure requirements and need not restate their financials as per US GAAP.

Otherwise prospectus has to be registered with SEC and disclosure requirements should be complied with and financials should be restated as per US GAAP.

Government approval should be taken for issue of ADR and special resolution to be passed as per section 81 of the Companies Act. Appointment of Lead Manager is important, since he has to take the firm through maze of regulations and should advise regarding price and promotion strategy to make the issue successful. There are several international lead managers and they are asked to make presentation to assess suitability before selecting one among them as lead manager, this process is known as *beauty parade*.

Then a draft prospectus which contains all the disclosure details other than price is prepared and the price to be charged is assessed through various investor meets at leading financial centers. This process is called as *road show*.

Minimum 100 million Dollar capitalization is required before a firm can make ADR issue.

In spite of these hurdles many firms resort to ADR due to prestige and visibility it offers, depth of American Market as well as due to the fact that ADR being equity instrument exchange risk is borne by investors and usually investor mandates the custodian bank not to exercise voting rights. Thus ADR is equity without loss of control.

Then listing agreements are entered with stock exchanges where they are listed.

Given FF 4.5/\$ and FF 180/DM what is expected \$/DM rate?

$$\$/DM = \$/FF * FF/DM$$

$$= 1/4.5 * 180$$

$$= 40$$

Discuss the recent trend in International Security Market?

As per the recent trend developing countries equity are finding more acceptance. Increasingly, depository receipts are finding favour with institutional investor. This is especially true in the case of industries like software where ADRs and GDRs are finding favour with investor considering the competitive edge countries like India and China have in this sector. In spite of strict disclosure requirements prescribed by SEC many software companies from India is going for ADR market due to the prestige and visibility associated with it. Apart from this due to the recent Enron debacle and subsequent meltdown of American Security Market again money has started flowing to emerging markets which process was not there after South East Asian crisis through FII increasingly integrating emerging and developed markets.

Due to Enron and other scandals like WorldComm US disclosure requirements have increased in the form of Sarbanese & Oxley Act and increasing emphasis is placed on corporate governance by many countries including India.

Many of the developing countries stock markets have attained international efficiency in the form of screen based trading, rolling settlement, and introduction of derivatives facilitating increased international integration.

Centralized cash management system is a double edged sword for international working capital management, discuss with the help of suitable example.

1. A Multi-National Company will have many branches throughout the world. Thus it can have surplus in one Branch and deficit in other Branch. It can have receivable in one Branch and payable in other Branch. It can opt for both centralized or decentralized system of cash management, both have their advantages and disadvantages, that is why it is called as double edged sword.
2. By centralizing it can hedge the foreign exchange risk better through hedging. For example an American MNC may have branches both in England and France. If English branch has receivables in $ and French branch has payable in $ it can better manage exchange risk through centralized cash management by netting receivable against payable and hedging the net risk only.
3. Some Branches may have surplus and may search suitable short term avenues for investing the same, while other branches have shortage and will be borrowing at high cost. For example in the above example of English branch has shortage and French Branch has surplus if the Funds are Managed centrally then the English Branch can be lent out of surplus of French branch facilitating better treasury management.
4. But there are many disadvantages in the form of transaction cost, for example for every remittance outward and inward commission has to be incurred in the form of difference between buy sell rate.
5. Suppose there is withholding tax for any remittance from France that should be factored in the Centralized cash management.
6. By centralizing cash management the advantage of London being major financial centre of the world is lost to the UK Branch.
7. Some times exchange controls for remittance outside the country makes the policy of centralized cash management impossible.
8. In spite of electronic fund transfer many a time there are delays in transfer of fund from centralized pool making centralized cash management system impracticable.

Thus, the various advantages and disadvantages make centralized cash management system as a double edged sword.

Explain Nastro and Vastro Account.

Nastro account means account maintained by domestic Bank with it's Foreign correspondent. Vastro Account means account maintained by correspondent Bank with domestic Bank.

Distinguish between the concept of reciprocal rate and cross rate with suitable examples.

For example if Rs/$ rate = 46Rs /$, then the reciprocal rate that is $/ Rs rate is

$/ Rs = 1/46= .02174$, this can be more clearly explained by dual rate concept

Rs/$= 46/46.50 then reciprocal rate is

$/ Rs= 1/46.5/1/46

= .02151/.02174

This can be theoretically explained that if the market wants to buy $ it has to pay 46.50 Rs inverse of which is Rs $ buying rate, if the market wants to sell $ it will get 46 Rs inverse of which is $/Rs sell rate.

While cross rate or synthetic rate in which exchange rate of one currency is determined through other currency.

For example if Rs/$ rate is 46/46.5, $/PS rate is 1.70/1.71 then Rs/PS rate is determined through synthetic or cross rate.

Rs/PS= Rs/$ * $/PS

= 46* 1.70/46.5*1.71

= 78.2/79.52

Write a note on

i. Purchasing Power Parity

ii. Interest Rate Parity.

Purchasing power parity

Purchasing power parity states that the exchange rate difference between two currencies is nothing but difference in inflation rate between two countries. Thus the currency of country with higher inflation will depreciate while country of currency with lower inflation will appreciate; otherwise there is scope for arbitrage.

But purchasing power parity theory suffers from several defects like.

1. Inflation index in different countries are measured based on different set of goods and services which are not comparable.
2. Purchasing power parity theory assumes absence of transaction cost or taxes which are unrealistic.

3. Purchasing power parity theory assumes absence of tariff and non-tariff barrier which is unrealistic.
4. Purchasing power parity theory assumes perfect market and absence of knowledge barrier which is unrealistic.
5. Purchasing power parity theory will be valid only if fundamental forces like Central Bank and Government dominate the market and not by speculators, since speculators will pump in hot money into economy if there is high inflation in anticipation of rise in interest rate.

Because of this there is not much empirical evidence supporting purchasing power parity theory.

Interest Rate Parity

Interest rate parity theory explains that the difference between exchange rate is due to difference between interest rate in two countries, otherwise there is scope for arbitrage.

Currency of the country having higher interest rate will depreciate and currency of country having lower interest rate will appreciate due to covered interest arbitrage. A person will borrow in a currency which has lower interest rate and due to increase in demand it will appreciate and deposit in currency with higher interest rate and due to higher interest rate it will depreciate. Interest rate parity theory assumes absence of transaction cost and taxes and exchange controls are not factored.

What do you mean by repatriation benefit?

In the case of countries with Exchange control, foreign exchange remittance is subject to approval by central Bank. But with a view to attract foreign capital the country can permit repatriation of principle, interest, dividend, sale proceeds of share in Foreign currency to attract foreign capital, this is called as repatriation benefit.

Explain the process of hedging against risk?

Hedging is a process to protect oneself against fluctuation in exchange rate against a spot transaction. There are several natural hedges like having exports and imports in the same currency. This is called as natural hedge. By invoicing in third currency hedging can be done. For example in the case of Indian Company $ being intervention currency the value of any other currency is done by crossing through dollar against other currencies. Thus, an Indian Company importing or exporting from Japan can hedge by invoicing in US$ instead of Japanese

Yen. But by this method it passes the exchange risk to other parties which the other party may agree or not.

Sometimes hedging will acquire strategic dimension when a country sources from another country to protect against appreciating local currency. Extreme form of this form of hedging is investing outside the country.

Hedging can also be done by using derivatives like Forwards, Futures, Options, and Swaps.

Thus, by hedging an uncertainty is converted to certainty, thereby eliminating risk, as a corollary return is also reduced.

Explain briefly the important strategies of direct investment in the context of international investment.

1. To overcome product life cycle: A product will undergo various life cycles like introduction, growth, maturity and decline. During maturity stage investment will move abroad in search of new market and growth.
2. To overcome tariff barrier: If heavy tariff barriers are imposed by importing country Foreign Direct investment is resorted to overcome the same.
3. To counter exchange rate appreciation: To overcome appreciating domestic currency investment will move to a country where currency appreciation is not much.
4. Due to availability of resources: Like in the case of cement unit investment will be located near limestone mines.
5. To protect technology: For example for companies like Coca Cola whose manufacturing process is secret investment will move abroad.
6. To protect brand equity: Companies like McDonald, Levis which have brand equity will establish regular outlets abroad instead of taking franchising route.
7. Following the customers: Big advertising agencies, multinational audit firms, multinational banks set up facilities wherever their customers go.
8. Transportation cost: Transportation cost which is heavy in the case of fragile items like glass will force multinational firm to set up manufacturing facility near the market.

List different types of swaps.

1. Interest rate swap between fixed and floating rate.
2. Swap between floating rate with different basis.
3. Exchange rate swap.
4. Forward rate agreement.

Explain the mechanism of currency trading.

A current trader acts as a broker as well as he takes position. The difference between buying and selling rate is the trader profit and it is called as spread. He thrives by buying low and selling high. He also takes positions in currencies, but generally intraday and overnight limits are fixed for such trading. Money is electronically transferred throughout the world in search of short term return. Currency traders also extensively deal in derivative market. Currency trader deals both in exchange traded market and OTC Market. Exchange is 24 hours business with New York, Frankfurt, Sydney, Bahrain, London, Singapore and Tokyo market. Huge volumes are there and many players operate in this market that is why it is called as perfect market.

The customer of a bank has requested to book a forward exchange contract for French Francs 8,50,000 for fixed delivery 6th Month.

Assuming French francs are quoted in London foreign exchange market against US dollars as under:

Spot US $ = 8.0700/8.0750 FFr.

3 month discount = .0950 .1050

6 month discount = .2300 .2500 and

US dollars are quoted in the local inter-bank exchange market as under:

Spot Rs.100 = 9.8000: 9.8025

3 Months discount = .0700 /.0725

6 months discount = .1300/.1325

What rate will Banker quote to the customer bearing in mind that Banker needs a cushion of .0500 on London rate, and exchange margin is .15% for TT selling and .2% for bill selling?

Spot US $ = 8.0700/8.0750 FFr

6th month forward rate = 8.0700+.2300: 8.0750+ .2500

= 8. 3000: 8.3250

Spot 100Rs = 9.8000: 9.8025

6th month forward rate = 9.8000+ .1300: 9.8025 + .1325

= 9.9300: 9.9350

Bank needs a cushion of .05 on London rate

So London rate $ = 8.2500: 8.2750 FF

FFr/ Rs. 100 = FFr/$* $/100Rs = 8.2500* 9.9300/ 8.2750* 9.9350

= 81.9225/ 82.2121

Since Forward transaction is given only for genuine trade transaction in India Bill selling rate will be applicable

So the Bank's rate is = 81.9225* .998/82.2121*.998

= 81.7587/ 82.0477

Rate quoted will be 81.7587 FFr for 100 Rs.

What is netting, how it improves MNCs performance?

Netting means offsetting the position in foreign exchange in one currency by a branch or subsidiary against opposite position in the same currency by another branch are subsidy and hedging the balance position only by centralized system of cash management. Since hedging involves cost to the organization by netting substantial savings can be achieved in the same.

Briefly explain different methods of exchange rate forecast and explain their suitability in Indian context.

Forward Rate as forecast: Forward can be said to be unbiased estimate of spot rate than accurate estimate since it involves premiums for predictable and unpredictable risk, out of which premium for unpredictable risk is difficult to estimate.

Balance of Payment Approach: Under this approach demand and supply determine the movement of the country.

Monetary Approach: This method is opposite of demand and supply approach that is when the GNP of country expands it leads to increase in exports and decrease in imports. It assumes constant money supply and full employment situation.

Portfolio Approach: Under this method when interest rate on bond increases currency appreciates to compensate the wealth increase.

Efficient Market Approach: Under this method past information is not useful in predicting future exchange rates. Actions of players like Government and central Bank as well as news should be used to predict future exchange rates.

Technical Analysis: Here patterns can be used to predict foreign exchange movements.

Fundamental Analysis: Here PPP & IRP are used to predict foreign exchange movement.

Out of this Fundamental Approach, Balance of Payment Approach and forward rates can be used as predictive tools in Indian context.

A currency swap has remaining life of 15 months. It involves exchanging interest at 14% on 20 million pounds for interest at 10% on 30 million $ once a year. The term structure of interest rates in UK and US is currently flat and if the swap were negotiated today the interest rate exchanged would be 8% in dollars and 11% in Sterling. All interest rates are quoted with annual compounding. The current Exchange rate is 1.6500. What is the value of the swap to the party paying Sterling? What is the value of swap to party paying $?

3 months later pound to be paid = 2.8 million pound/4 = .7 million pound.

15 months later pound to be paid = 2.8 million pounds + 20 million pounds = 22.8 million pounds

3 months later present value = .7 million pound + 22.8/1.11

= .7 million pounds + 20.54

= 21.24 million pounds

Present value= 21.24/(1.11/4) = 21.24/(1.0275) = 20.67 million pounds.

Value of $ swap 3 months hence = .75 million $+ 33 million $/(1.08)

= .75 million $ + 30.56 million $

= 31.31 million $.

Present value of swap = 31.31 / (1.02) = 30.70 million $

Conversion at current exchange rate to pound sterling = 30.7/1.65 = 18.60 million pounds.

Value of swap to party paying in pound sterling = 18.60–20.67= – 2.07 million pound sterling.

Value of dollar paying party = 30.7 – (20.67* 1.65)

= 30.7 – 34.11 = –3.41 million $.

11.8 MODEL PAPER VIII

What is the current account generally composed of?

Current account is generally composed of exports and imports of goods and services, transfer payments like gifts, pension, interest etc.

How exchange rate stability does affect international trade?

An exporter or importer has to pay in currency other than that of his own. Thus an appreciation or depreciation in exchange rate will have an effect on the payment in terms of domestic currency. Thus an appreciation in domestic currency will make imports cheaper and exports unattractive and vice versa is also true subject to elasticity of demand of goods.

Depreciation of domestic currency will increase the domestic inflation rate in the form of cost push inflation and this will make the domestic industry uneconomical. At the same time appreciation of currency will make the goods uncompetitive, thereby forcing domestic industries to relocate themselves to escape exchange rate appreciation and retain their competitiveness having an effect on domestic employment.

A stable exchange rate will attract foreign investment, while under instability Foreign investor will try to take out their money leading to further instability as it happened during South East Asian crisis in 1997.

The following data are given:

1. An exporter sells watches to Russia for Rs 50,000. The exporter accepts Rs 50,000 in cash and remaining as one year bill of exchange.

2. Mohan, an Indian, goes to Sri Lanka on vacation with Rs 2,000. He spent Rs 1000 on services received and bought souvenirs for Rs 900 to bring with him.
3. An Indian Company imports cloth worth Rs 5000 from Nepal.
4. Karim of Bangladesh immigrates to India with Rs 1000.
5. Karim finds a job and sends Rs 1500 to his family in Bangladesh
6. ABC Company of India decides to invest Rs 6,00,000 in Mauritius to establish a business unit. Half of this investment is made in cash; remaining half is arranged by selling bonds in France.
7. Profit made by Mauritian subsidiary of ABC Company is Rs 20,000 of which 25% is remitted to Parent Company in India.
8. The Government of Sri Lanka issued bonds worth Rs 50,000 with interest rate of 5%. Indians buy 20% of this bond.
9. An exporter, Madan, sells spare parts worth Rs 25,000 to Colombia and receives payment on delivery.
10. A US exporter sells to India a process equipment for Rs 1,50,000.
11. The Government of Sri Lanka paid interest of 5% on its bond.
12. Indian importer paid Rs 2,500 to an English Shipping Company as charges.
13. Karim sold some of his property to Bangladesh for Rs 5,000. His family members paid Rs 1000 to Air India for travel and the remaining amount they bought in cash.

Prepare a table of source and use of Funds.

Write down various Sub Balances (in INR).

Item no.	Particulars	Source	Uses
1.	Current Account		5,00,000
	Capital Account		4,50,000
2.	Services Current Account		1,000
	Imports Current Account		900
3.	Current Account Import		5,000
4.	Transfer receipt current a/c		1,000
5.	Transfer Payments		1,500

Item no.	Particulars	Source	Uses
6.	FDI Capital Account		6,00,000
7.	FDI Capital Account		3,00,000
8.	Services Dividend current a/c		5,000
9.	FDI Capital Account		10,000
10.	Exports Current Account		25,000
11.	Imports current a/c		1,50,000
12.	Service – Current a/c		2,500
13.	Service- Current Account		2,500
14.	Services Current Account		1,000
15.	Transfer payment current a/c		4,000

Positive Balance of Rs. 3,72,600 in Current account.

Negative Balance in capital account Rs. 7,40,000.

What do you mean by SDR?

SDR is Special Drawing Rights introduced by IMF after the oil shock to shore up international liquidity. SDR is not a currency but a basket having weightage of different actively traded currencies. Any member can exchange it's own currency against SDR up to twice the amount of his quota. SDR is a virtual currency which can be used for buying another currency and not for payment for goods. Since it consists of a basket of currencies it is more stable than any single currency.

You are setting up a project in USA. The estimated NPV is $ 12v million. Your Finance office stated in the report that he had not accounted for Foreign Exchange Risk. He felt that with such large NPV, the project should be accepted since a risk adjusted NPV is likely to be positive. You have the Final decision to accept or reject the project. What is your decision?

International Projects are characterized by high risk which is what distinguishes international project from local projects. So there is no scope for intendment in risk whatever may be the positive NPV. International projects are characterized by country risk that means country imposing restrictions on transfer of profit and capital. Extreme forms of country risks are nationalization and expropriation. Apart from this exchange fluctuation is also a risk. These risks may get compounded thereby making total risk very high.

In international Project Appraisal these risks are unbundled, all equity rate is established depending on the risk level. Highly risky cash flows are discounted at these rates, Tax benefits due to Depreciation, interest on borrowings are discounted at risk free rates depending on their level of certainty, benefit due to concessional lending are also taken into effect, exchange fluctuation is factored.

This method of unbundling risk based on the different levels of risks and finding out the net cash flow is called as Adjusted Present Value.

Thus without doing such an analysis one cannot accept or reject the project.

Calculate the following rates into outright sales.

Indicate the spread.

Calculate the annualized bid ask premium or discount over spot rate.

	Spot	1month	3 month	6 month
Rs/ Dollar	35.6300/25	20/25	25/35	30/40
Rs/ Pound	55. 2200/35	40/30	50/35	55/42
Rs/ DM	23.9000/30	30/25	40/60	45/65
Rs/ $	35.6300/35.6325	35.6320/35.6325	35.6325/35.6335	35.6330/35.6340
		.067%/.084	.028%/.039%	.017%/.022%
Rs/Pound	55.2200/55.2235	55.2160/55.2205	55.2150/ 55.2200	55.2145/ 55.2148
		–.0869%/.065%	.036%/.025%	–.019%/.015%
Rs/DM	23.9000/23.9035	23.8970/ 23.8975	23.9040/ 23.9060	23.9045/ 23.9065
		–.15%/.1255%	.067%/.1%	.038%/.054%

Explain International Fischer effect.

International Fischer effect says that the difference between exchange rates is due to difference in real interest rate, which is nominal interest rate adjusted for inflation rate. Ultimately real interest rate will converge across the world as per international Fischer effect.

Derive and explain monetary approach.

Under Monetary approach if the real GNP of the country increases then if the money supply do not increase then since less money is chasing more goods process of the goods will fall and PPP will operate and due to fall in inflation Exchange rate of the currency will appreciate. This is exactly as opposed to theory of demand and supply as propounded by Balance of Payment approach.

The correction for the same will come due to less availability of money there will not be any purchase of bonds due to which the demand for bonds will fall thereby reducing price and increasing interest rate. Due to increase in interest rate holding stock of money will become unattractive thereby more goods will be purchased leading to inflation and consequent depreciation in value of currency to correct appreciation.

Thus monetary approach unlike PPP says that the money supply itself causes appreciation or depreciation much before inflation as propounded by PPP.

While you were visiting London, you purchased a Jaguar for 35,000 Pounds, payable in three months. You have enough cash at your bank in New York City, which pay .35% interest per month, compounding monthly, to pay for the car. Currently the spot exchange rate is 1.45$ / pound and the three month forward rate is 1.40$/ pound in London, the money market interest rate is 2% for a three month investment. There are two alternative ways of paying for your Jaguar.

1. **Keep the funds at your bank in the United States and buy Pound Sterling 35,000 forward.**
2. **Buy certain pound amount spot today and invest the amount in UK for three months so that the maturity value becomes equal to 35,000. Evaluate each payment method. Which method you prefer? Why?**

If forward is booked after 3 months 35000* 1.40$ to be paid = 49,000$

Present value of the same is = 49000/ (1.0035) ^3= 48490$.

If dollar has to be converted to pound sterling number of $ required now is 35000/(1.02) = 34314 Pound sterling.

$ = 34314*1.45 = 49755 $

Thus Forward route being cheaper is better.

Who are the participants in the Foreign Exchange Market?

Participants in Foreign Exchange Markets are corporates, Central Banks of the countries, brokers, Bankers, speculators.

Consider the following data.

	Exchange rates	$ interest rate	Pound interest rate
Spot	$ 1.5753		
1 month	$ 1.5623	3% pa	8.5% pa
3 months	$ 1.5577	3.5% pa	7.5% pa
6 months	$ 1.5536	3.5% pa	7% pa

1. Find out the arbitrage possibilities for various periods.
2. Show how interest parity will be restored as a result of arbitrage activities?

1. 1 month forward rate as per interest rate arbitrage theory is
   1.5753*(1.0025)/(1.0071)
   = 1.5681

   Thus, as per interest rate parity Forward premium is underpriced in terms off dollar. An arbitrageur will purchase pound one month against Dollar.
2. 3 month forward premium as per interest arbitrage theory is
   1.5753*(1.0088)/((1.0188)= 1.5598

   So forward rate is underpriced in terms of $. One pound can be purchased forward against 1.5577$ for third month and three month later it can be sold for 1.5598 $ and the arbitrageur can make 1.5598–1.5577 = .0021$ per pound.
3. 6 month forward rate as per interest rate parity theory
   a * (1.0175)/(1.035)= 1.5487$.

Thus, pound is over valued. Sell pound six months forward. After six months one pound can be procured by an arbitrageur at 1.5487$ and can be delivered against forward contact and 1.5536$ can be obtained, thereby riskless profit of .0049 $ per pound can be made.

Thus by performing above arbitrage activities Demand for pound one month and three months will increase and thereby pound value will increase till it reaches the interest parity level of 1.5681 and 1.5598 $ for first and third month respectively.

For six months due to sale of pound the value of pound will decline till the sixth month pound reaches interest parity level of 1.5487$.

It is, generally, not possible to completely eliminate both translation and transaction exposure. In some cases, the elimination of one exposure will also eliminate other. But in other cases elimination of one exposure actually creates other. Discuss which exposure might be viewed as the most important to effectively manage, if conflict between controlling both arises.

Transaction exposure is also called as contract exposure. It is short term in nature. It involves actual cash flow. Translation exposure does not involve cash flow but for tax related cash flow. It only affects the Balance sheet since the foreign currency denominated asset or liability should be incorporated in the parent entities Balance Sheet at local rates.

For example a credit sales creates transaction as well as translation exposure. In this case hedging against transaction exposure by any one of the means like forward, option or future acts as hedge against translation exposure.

But if the transaction exposure like payment for creditors is sought to be hedged by keeping a foreign currency deposit as a money market hedge, this eliminates transaction exposure but creates translation exposure.

If transaction exposure in the form of foreign currency payment in exports is sought to be eliminated by creating foreign branch it actually creates translation exposure.

If conflict between both exposure then transaction exposure has to be managed effectively since this involves actual outflow of cash, thereby the firm's solvency is endangered.

Define Translation exposure.

Translation exposure is also called as accounting exposure. It is there due to holding foreign currency assets and liabilities. It does not involve any cash outflow other than tax related.

Discuss the Advantage and disadvantage of maintaining multiple manufacturing sites in various countries as hedge against exchange rate exposure.

Exchange rate risk can be minimized by setting up manufacturing sites in various countries and invoicing in various currencies, thereby the adverse effect on operations due to appreciation or depreciation of exchange rate can be managed.

Companies in Japan expanded in South East Asian countries during 80s to ward off the threat to the cost structure of its industry due to appreciating yen. Thus, many tiger economies emerged.

But this method only converts transaction exposure to translation exposure. That is the effect of exchange rate fluctuation is recorded in the Balance Sheet of parents at the time of closing of books. Even though translation exposure is recorded in the books of the company it is disallowed for tax purposes in many countries.

But diversifying in different countries leads to country risks in the form of blocked accounts, nationalization, adverse policies like discriminatory taxation and in certain circumstances it can take extreme forms like expropriation.

Suppose that you hold a piece of land in the city of London that you may want to sell in one year. As a US resident, you are concerned with the dollar value of the land. Assume that, if the British Economy booms in future, the land will be worth 2000 pound sterling and one British pound will be worth \$ 1.40. If the British Economy slows down on the other hand, the land will be worth less say 1500 PS, but the pound will be stronger say 1.50\$/ pound. You feel that the British economy will experience a boom of 60% probability and slowdown 40% probability.

1. Estimate your exposure to Exchange risk.
2. Compute the variance of \$ value of property that is attributable to exchange rate uncertainty.
3. Discuss how you can handle exchange risk exposure and the consequence of hedging.

Average value of property = 2000* .60 + 1500* .40= 1800 pounds

Average exchange rate = 1.40*.6+ 1.50*.4= 1.44 $.

Average value = 1800* 1.44= 2592

If the British Economy booms value = 2000*1.40= 2800$

Exposure = 2800–2592/(1.40–1.44) =208/ (–.04)= –5200$ thus the exposure is more than the value of the asset.

If the British Economy slows down

Exposure value of the asset = 1500* 1.50= 2250$

Change in $ value = 2250-2592= –342$

Change in exchange rate = 1.50–1.44= .06$/pound

Exposure = –342/.06= –5700$ is more than the value of asset.

Variance due to $ value

Variance due to exchange rate uncertainty = (–5200) * (–5200) * (.04)(.04)

= 27040000 * .0016= 43264

Variance due to exchange rate uncertainty = (–5700) * (–5700) * (.06)(.06) = 116964

Exchange risk exposure can be hedged through netting that is creating assets and liabilities in the same currencies. But this may not eliminate timing difference that is difference in timing for payment of assets and liabilities. Money market hedge, or through derivatives like forwards, futures, options and swaps through which the risks can be successfully transferred. But these instruments have an element of risk premium for unexpected changes and to that extent the organization has to incur costs if the unexpected change does not take place or even if taking place is not to the extent anticipated.

An importer has purchased from France goods worth 50,000 FFr. There are no quotes available for rupee versus FFr. The quotes available are US$ = Rs 35.000/ 35.080 and US$ = FFr. 5.1025/5.1050. What is the value of transaction in Rupee terms?

Rs/ FFr = Rs/$ *$/FFr.

= 35* 1/5.1050./ 35.080/ 5.1025= 6.8560/ 6.8751.

Indian importer has to sell 6.8751 Rs to get one FFr assuming no commission.

Total payment by Indian importer = 50,000FFr* 6.8751 = 343755Rs.

Identify factors to be considered in assessing country risk. Briefly elaborate how each factor can affect the risk to MNC.

The factors that are considered in assessing country risks are availability of natural resources as well as skilled human resources. For example many countries want to shift their back office to India due to availability of English educated, computer literate manpower.

Existence of proper infrastructure like proper and stable government, sound and independent legal systems, infrastructure like port, roads, accommodations etc. are favourably considered in assessing country risk. Knowledgeable officials in Government, encouragement to private enterprise are considered favourable in assessing country risk.

External factors like exchange rate, current account position, foreign exchange reserves, stable fiscal policies are all considered favourably in assessing country risk.

Proper Fiscal and monetary policies, non-discriminatory taxation, absence of terrorism, revolution, absence of threat to international investment like Nationalization, blocked accounts, expropriations are important factors of country risk.

There are several credit agencies like Standard & Poor, Moody who specialize in assessing country risk, even though they have been accused of being biased in their assessment against developing countries.

Cray Research sold a super computer to Max Planc Institute in Germany on credit and invoiced DM 10 Million payable in six months. Currently, the six month forward exchange rate is DM 1.50 /$ and the Foreign Exchange adviser for Cray Research predicts that the spot rate is likely to be DM 1.43/$ in six months.

1. **What is the expected gain/loss from a forward hedge?**
2. **If you are the Finance Manager of Cray Research, would you recommend hedging this DM receivable? Why or why not?**
3. **Suppose the Foreign Exchange adviser predicts that the future spot rate will be same as the forward exchange rate quoted today. Would you recommend hedging in this case, why or why not?**

1. Expected loss will be 10000000/ 1.50 = 66,66,667 $ – (10000000 / 1.43) = 6993007 = 326340$.
2. If I am the Finance Manager then I will not recommend this hedge since such a policy will lead to loss in terms of $ due to DM appreciating against dollar.
3. If the Foreign Exchange adviser predicts that the forward rate will be same as spot rate, Hedging is advisable to guard against future unexpected changes. But the downside is that if there is favourable movement of exchange rates then the benefit is lost to the company. But forward rates do not have any upfront costs.

But in Foreign exchange market where unexpected changes occur in random manner nobody can predict accurately, thus partial hedging or hedging with flexibility like options which involve upfront premium can be employed depending on the extent of certainty as perceived in this prediction by the management.

a. List one situation when Multinational Corporation is exposed to interest rate risk.

b. As an investor, what factors would you consider before investing in the emerging stock market of a developing country?

c. Describe some potential benefits to MNC as a result of Direct Foreign Investment.

a. Suppose a Multinational Company is engaged in decentralized cash management then if one unit borrows a currency at fixed rate, while other unit lends the same currency at floating rate as a part of treasury operations, MNC is exposed to interest rate risk.

b. Emerging Market investments are taken as a measure of portfolio diversification, to increase return without correspondingly increasing the risk as per Markowitz portfolio theory, since emerging market and developed markets are not perfectly correlated, due to exchange control, information asymmetry. Emerging market offers higher returns with corresponding higher risk, while in developed market being matured market risk is low but at the same time return is low.

Investor investing in emerging market has to assess the level of risk he has to take. He should assess the country risk if the country in which he proposes to invest.

In considering country risk he should assess the natural as well as human resource and find out whether the Sector in which he is investing has unique strength like software in India. He should also track government policies like fiscal, monetary policies, institutions like stable government, sound and fair judicial system, infrastructure, track record of the country in levying discriminatory taxes on foreign investment, nationalization, expropriation, and exchange control.

He should also assess the strengths of the company he wants to invest in.

If he is not able to do the assessment he can route his investment through mutual funds.

Describe some potential benefits to MNC as a result of direct foreign investments. Elaborate on each type of benefits.

Potential benefits to MNC from FDI are:

- Risk reduction without a corresponding reduction in risk.
- Cost reduction.
- To get over the problem of appreciation of exchange rate.
- To get over tariff barriers.
- To exploit natural resources.
- To keep proprietary technology secret.
- To exploit brand equity.
- To divert the attention of foreign competitors.
- Following customers.

a. Since various markets in the world are not perfectly correlated by FDI a firm can reduce risk without correspondingly reducing the return.

b. For example Japan relocated manufacturing facilities in South Korea, Thailand etc. being low cost centers, thereby leading to their tiger status.

c. Many countries relocate manufacturing facility due to appreciating exchange rates to make them competitive.

d. Many FDI was done in India to get over high tariff barriers.

e. FDIs in African countries takes place due to availability of natural resources like copper etc. Many multinationals get located in Middle East to exploit crude oil.

f. Coca cola establishes 100% subsidiaries throughout the world to protect its manufacturing formula which is secret.

g. McDonald, Levi etc. are setting up FDI throughout the world to leverage on their name.

h. Sometimes a company sets operations in the country of it's foreign competitors to divert their attention like US companies setting shop in Japan.

i. Advertisement agencies, international audit firms and some Japanese suppliers to maintain JIT system follow their customers to whichever country they go to maintain their relationship.

CASE STUDY

The Sports Exports Company converts British pounds into dollars every month. The prevailing spot rate is about $ 1.65 but there is much uncertainty about the future value of the pound. Jim Logan, Owner of the Sports Exports Company, expects that British inflation will rise substantially in the future. In the previous year when the British inflation was high, pound depreciated. The prevailing British interest rate is slightly higher than the prevailing U.S. interest rate. The pound has risen slightly over each of the last several months; Jim wants to forecast the value of the pound for each of the next 20 months.

1. Explain how Jim could use technical forecasting to forecast the future value of the pound. Based on the information provided, do you think that a technical forecast of the pound would reflect future appreciation in the Pound?
2. Explain how Jim could use fundamental forecasting the future value of the pound. Based on the information provided, do you think that a fundamental forecast of the pound would reflect appreciation or depreciation of the Pound?
3. Explain how Jim could use a market based forecast the future value of the pound. Do you think the market based forecast would reflect appreciation, depreciation, or no change in the value of pound?

Does it appear that all the forecast techniques will lead to the same forecast of the pound future value? What forecast technique would you prefer to use in this situation?

1. Technical analysis does not depend upon theories like PPP or interest rate parity to predict the value of exchange rate. They plot the exchange rate and based on historical pattern predict future behavior. Thus, here the historical facts suggested that British pound

depreciated when the inflation was high, based on the same under technical analysis it can be predicted that pound will depreciate.

2. Under Fundamental analysis based on Purchasing Power Parity principle higher the inflation the currency will depreciate or interest rate parity principle higher the interest rate the currency will depreciate, under international Fischer effect real interest rate that is interest rate adjusted for inflation to be used for determining the interest rate parity theory it can be expected that pound will depreciate.
3. In market based approach since foreign exchange market is an efficient market it reflects all the available historical data as well as expected data, while unexpected data occur in a purely random manner, so historical data cannot be used as the measure of predicting future value. Even though foreign exchange market.
4. It consists of many players and all of them act on profit motive, central Bank of a country and Government do not act on profit motive, thus to this extent the market is not efficient. Thus, Government should use the data of the country's fiscal balance, money supply to predict the movement of exchange rate. Since the future inflation is expected to be high Britain will try to reduce the fiscal deficit, control money supply, and increase interest rate which may lead to appreciation of pound or at least arrest the extent of depreciation of pound.
5. All will not yield same results since the basis is different. With the given data we can use fundamental analysis to predict the value of exchange rate than any other technique.

Glossary

Absolute purchasing Power Theory: A version of PPP theory explaining that the relationship between domestic and foreign price levels under floating exchange rate regime equals the equilibrium exchange rate between the two currencies.

Accounting exposure: The amount of foreign exchange exposure reflected in a company's financial statements.

American Depository Receipts (ADRs): Claims issued against foreign shares and traded in the over-the counter market. ADRs are used so that the foreign shares can trade in their home market but nevertheless be sold in the United States.

American option: Options exercised even before maturity.

Arbitrage: Simultaneously buying and selling for the purpose of profiting from price differences. It involves making risk free profits.

Arm's length price: The price at which a seller transacts with an unrelated buyer. Normally, it is based on cost/market price.

Arm's-length pricing: Prices set according to proper market values. See administered prices and transfer prices.

Asis risk: Relate primarily to financial companies, it arises when interest rate exposure on one instrument is not fully offset by the interest rate exposure on the other instrument.

At the money: It denotes a position in the options market where strike rate is equal to the spot rate.

Balance of payments: A Marco-level statement showing inflow and outflow of foreign exchange on different account.

Balance of trade: A commonly used abbreviation for the balance on (merchandise) trade and equal to merchandise exports minus merchandise imports.

Balance of trade: The difference between the value of export and import of merchandise.

Banker's acceptance: A time draft drawn on and accepted by a commercial bank.

Basis point: Equal to 1/100 of one percent.

Basis risk: The risk of unexpected change in the relationship between futures and spot prices.

Basis Swap: A floating-for-floating interest rate swap that pairs two floating rate instruments at different maturities (such as six-month LIBOR versus thirty day U.S. Treasury Bills)

Basis: The simple difference between two nominal interest rates.

Bid rate: The rate at which a market maker is willing to buy the quoted asset.

Bill of lading: A document involving contract between the exporter and carrier for the shipment of goods. It serves as a receipt for the exporter.

Black-Scholes model: A model developed in 1973 for measuring the value of currency options,

Blocked funds: Cash flows generated by a foreign project that cannot be immediately repatriated to the parent firm because of capital flow restrictions imposed by the host government.

Bretton Woods system: The procedure for fixing exchange rates and managing the international financial system, worked out in Bretton Woods, New Hampshire, in 1944. The system involved fixing foreign currencies to the U.S. Dollar, and the U.S. Dollar to gold. The Bretton Woods system was in effect until the early 1970s. Also called the gold exchange standard.

Bulldog bond: A bond issued in the UK by a non-resident.

Call option: The right to buy the underlying currency at a specified price an on a specified date.

Cartellisation: Cartellisation offers small number of producers; the members jointly determine the policy jointly. For example Oil prices are decided as a result of cartellisation by OPEC.

Clearing house automated payments system (CHAPS): A network of UK banks with computer-operated payments settlement system.

Clearing House Interbank Payments System (CHIPS): The clearing house used to settle inter bank transactions in which the foreign exchange purchases and sales settled in U.S. Dollars. CHIPS is located in New York and is owned by its members.

Commodity swap: A swap in which the (often notional) principal amount on at least one side of the swap is a commodity such as oil or gold.

Comparative advantage: A relative efficiency in producing something, indicated by having a lower opportunity cost of one product versus another product than occurs in some other Country. Countries gain from International trade by producing products for which they have a comparative advantage. See absolute advantage.

Countervailing Duty: Taxes applied to offset measures that other countries have take to make their goods artificially cheap, such as export subsidies or dumping.

Country risk: The political and financial risks of conducting business in particular foreign country.

Coupon swap: A fixed-for-floating interest rate swap.

Crawling peg: An automatic system for revising the parity (par) exchange rate, typically basing the par value on recent experience of the actual exchange rate within its support points. The crawling pet allows exchange rates to move toward equilibrium levels in the long run while reducing functions in the short run.

Cross-hedge: A futures hedge using a currency that is different from, but closely related to, the currency of the underlying exposure.

Currency coupon swap: A fixed-for-floating rate non-amortizing currency swap traded primarily through international commercial bank.

Currency cross-hedge: A hedge of currency risk using a currency that is correlated with the currency in which the underlying exposure is denominated.

Currency option: A contract giving the option holder the right to buy or sell an underlying currency at a specified price and on a specified date. The option writer (seller) holds the obligation to fulfill the other side of the contract.

Currency swap: One borrowed currency is exchanged for the other in order to avail of the desired currency. This is done through the swap dealer.

Depository receipt: A derivative security issued by a foreign borrower through a domestic trustee representing ownership in deposit foreign shares.

Derivative security: A financial security whose price is derived from the price of another assets.

Dirty float: Occurs when governments attempt to influence exchange rates which are otherwise flexible and allowed to float. Also called a managed float.

Economic exposure: A more complete title for exposure, with the word "economic" added to distinguish true economic effects of exchange rates from effects which appear in financial statements. Effects in financial statements involve accounting exposure.

Economies of scale: Achieving lower average cost per unit through a larger scale of production.

Escrow account: An account which a bank holds in the name of third party for specific purpose.

Eurobonds: Fixed rate Euro currency deposits and loans and Eurocurrencies with maturity longer than five years.

Eurocurrencies: Deposits and loans denominated in one currency and traded in a market outside the borders of the country issuing that currency (e.g., Euro dollars).

European currency unit (ECU): A trade-weighted basket of currencies in the European Exchange Rate Mechanism (ERM) of the European Union.

European Exchange rate mechanism (ERM): The exchange rate system used by countries in the European Union in which exchange rates are pegged within bands around an ERM central value.

European Monetary System (EMS): An exchange rate system based on cooperation between European Union central banks.

European Union (EU): Formerly the European Economic Community, a regional trade pact that includes Belgium ,France, Germany, Italy, the Netherlands, Portugal, Spain and the United Kingdom (England, Wales, Northern Ireland, and Scotland)

Expropriation: A specific type of political risk in which a government seizes foreign assets.

Expropriation: The seizure of assets with compensation. See confiscation.

Factor model: A model that assumes a linear relation between an asset's expected return and one or more systematic risk factors.

Factoring: Sale of an accounts receivable balance to buyers (factors) that are willing and able to bear the costs and risks of credit and collections.

Financial Engineering: The process of innovation by which new financial products are created.

Financial price risk: The risk of unexpected changes in financial price, including currency (foreign exchange) risk interest rate risk, and commodity price risk.

Financial risk: Financial risk refers to unexpected events in a country's financial, economic, or business life.

Fisher effect: The closed version of the theory explaining that nominal interest rate combines both the real interest rate and the rate of inflation ; while the open version of the theory explaining that inflation rate differential between the two countries equals the nominal interest rate differential between them.

Foreign direct investment (FDI): The act of building productive capacity directly jn a foreign country.

Foreign exchange (currency) risk: The risk of unexpected changes in foreign currency exchanged rates.

Foreign exchange exposure: The sensitivity of changes in the real domestic-currency value of assets, liabilities, or operating incomes to unanticipated changes in exchange rates. Exposure can be measured by the slope of a regression equation which relates changes in values of assets, liabilities, or operating incomes to unanticipated changes in exchange rates.

Forfaiting: A form of medium-term no recourse exports financing. Involves a series of avaled time drafts.

Forward contract: A commitment to exchange a specified amount of one currency for a specified amount of another currency on a specified future date.

Forward market: A market for forward contracts in which trades are made for future delivery according to an agreed-upon delivery date, exchange rate, and amount.

Forward premium: A currency whose nominal value in the forward market is higher than in the spot market. (Contrast with forward discount)

Fundamental analysis: A method of predicting exchange rates using the relationships of exchange rates to fundamental economic variables such as GNP growth, money supply and trade balances.

G-7 nations: Seven major industrialised countries, viz. Germany, France, Italy, the UK, Canada, Japan and the USA.

General Agreement on Tariffs and Trade (GATT): A worldwide trade agreement designed to reduce tariffs, it was incorporated in 1948.

Global bond: A bond that trades in the Eurobond market as well as in one or more national bond markets.

Hard Currency: A freely convertible currency not easily expected to depreciate.

Hedge funds: Private investment partnerships with a general manager and several limited partners.

Hedge: A position or operation that offset an underlying exposure.

Index futures: A futures contract that allows investors to buy or sell an index (such as a foreign stock index) in the futures market.

Index options: A call or put option contract on an index (Such as a foreign stock market index)

Index Swap: A swap of a market index for some other asset (such as a stock-for-stock or debt-for-stock swap)

Informational efficiency: Whether or not market prices reflect information and thus the true (or intrinsic) value of the underlying asset.

Integrated financial Market: A market in which there are no barriers to financial flows and purchasing power parity holds across equivalent assets.

Intellectual property rights: Patents, copyrights, and proprietary technologies and processes that are the basis of the multinational corporation's competitive advantage over local firms.

Interbank spread: The difference between a bank's offer and bid rates for deposits in the Eurocurrency market.

Interest rate risk: The risk of unexpected changes in an interest rate.

Interest rate swap: An agreement to exchange interest payments for a specific period of time on a given principal amount. the most common interest rate swap is a fixed-for-floating coupon swap. The notional principal is typically not exchanged.

International bonds: Bonds that are traded outside the country of the issuer. International bonds are either foreign bonds trading in a foreign national market or Eurobonds trading in the international market.

In-the-money option: An option that has value if exercised immediately.

Intrinsic value of an option: The value of an option of exercised immediately.

Lead manager: The lead investment bank in a syndicate selling a public securities offering.

Leading and lagging: The practice of netting receivables and payables over a period of time forward, called leading, and backward, called lagging.

Letter of credit (L/C): An irrevocable guarantee from a bank that a seller's credit to a buyer will be honored provided the seller fulfills her or his part of a specified agreement, such as the delivery of documents called for in the letter of credit

London inter bank offer rate (LIBOR): Interest rate charged on inter bank loans in London. The average of rates charged by large, London banks on a given currency of often used as the basis for adjusting interest rates on floating-rate loans.

London inter-bank bid rate (LIBID): The interest rate at which major banks in London bid to accept deposit from one another for a given maturity.

Money market hedge: A hedge that replicates a currency forward contract through the spot currency and Eurocurrency markets.

Money markets: Markets for financial assets and liabilities of short maturity, usually less than one year.

Netting: Calculating the overall situations for payables and receivables in a currency that faces a firm. Amounts to be paid are subtracted from amounts to be received so that hedging can be limited to the net amount of the currency coming in or going out. See leading and lagging.

Operating exposure: The sensitivity of changes in the real domestic-currency value of operating incomes to unanticipated changes in exchange rates. Also called residual foreign exchange exposure or Economic Exposure.

Political risk: The risk that a sovereign host government will unexpectedly change the rules of the game under which businesses operate. Political risk includes both macro and micro risks.

Price elasticity of demand: The sensitivity of quantity sold to a percentage change in price (-%q/%p).

Purchasing power parity (law of one price): The principle that equivalent assets sell for the same price. Purchasing power parity is enforced in the currency markets by financial market arbitrage.

Purchasing-power parity (PPP) principle: The idea that exchange rates are determined by the amounts of different currencies required to purchase a representative bundle of goods.

Put option: The right to sell the under lying asset at a specified price and on a specified dated.

Put-call parity: The relation of the value of a long call, a short put, the exercise price, and the forward price at expiration;

Random Walk: A process in which instantaneous changes in exchange rates are normally distributed with a zero mean and constant variance.

Repatriation: Bringing funds home from abroad.

Rollover (swap): A swap where the purchase/sale and subsequent sale/purchase of a currency are separated by 1 business day.

Short position: A position in which a particular asset (such as spot or forward currency) has been sold.

Short selling: Selling an asset that you do not own or taking a short position.

Special Drawing Rights (SDRs): Reserves at, and created by, the International Monetary Fund (IMF) and allocated by making ledger entries in countries' accounts at the IMF. Used for meeting imbalances in the balance of payments and assisting developing nations.

Spot market: A market in which trades are made for immediate delivery (within two business days for most spot currencies.)

Swap (currency): A sale/purchase of a currency combined with an offsetting purchase / sale for a later time, or borrowing and lending in the same currency. The initial purchase/sale might be a spot transaction, with the offsetting sale/purchase being a forward transaction. This is a spot forward swap. However there are also forward-forward swaps involving offsetting purchases and sales where all transactions occur in the future. See outright forward contract, swap-in, and swap-out.

SWIFT (Society for World wide Interbank Financial Transactions): Network through which international banks conduct their financial transactions.

Tariff: A tax on imports.

Time value of an option: The difference between the value of an option and the option's intrinsic value.

Total risk: The sum of systematic and unsystematic risk measured by the standard deviation or variance of return).

Transaction cost: The amount paid in brokerage or similar charges when making a transaction. On currencies, transaction costs are represented by the spread between the bids and ask exchange rates.

Transaction Exposure: Changes in exchange rate causing changes in the present cash flow.

Transfer price: Arbitrarily determined price normally for intra-firm transfer of goods and services which is quite different from arm's-length price and which is done for the purpose of reducing overall tax and tariff burden as also for the working capital management.

Withholding tax: A tax on dividend or interest income that is withheld for payment of taxes in a host country. Payment is typically withheld by the financial institution distributing the payment.

World Trade Organisation (WTO): Created in 1994 by 121 nations at the Uruguay round of the General Agreement on Tariffs and Trade (GATT). The WTO is responsible for implementation and administration of the trade agreement.